THE BEST OF BRIDGE

Royal Treats For Entertaining

FIRST EFFORT
FOURTEENTH TIME 'ROUND

WRITTEN AND PUBLISHED BY:
BEST OF BRIDGE PUBLISHING LIMITED
CALGARY, ALBERTA, CANADA.
PRINTED BY CENTAX OF CANADA
HAND LETTERED BY NORM W. HODGINS
PHOTOGRAPHY BY COMMERCIAL ILLUSTRATORS LTD.
COPYRIGHT © 1980 BY BEST OF BRIDGE PUBLISHING LTD.

ISBN 0-9690425-0-7

OUR THANKS

MANY RECIPES COLLECTED HEREIN HAVE BEEN HANDED DOWN WITHIN OUR FAMILIES. MANY OTHERS HAVE BEEN PASSED FROM FRIEND TO FRIEND - THE ORIGINAL SOURCE LONG SINCE FORGOTTEN. WE HAVE USED EACH RECIPE TIME AND AGAIN AND WE TRUST YOU WILL ENJOY BOTH SERVING AND MAKING THEM FOR YOUR FRIENDS, EITHER AT BRIDGE, AS LUNCHEONS OR AS A LATE EVENING SNACK. WE WISH TO THANK OUR PALS FOR THEIR SUPPORT AND ESPECIALLY OUR HUSBANDS, WHO, THOUGH LAUGHING, ENCOURAGED US IN THIS WOMEN'S YEAR. HAPPY ENTERTAINING!!

KAREN BRIMACOMBE

LINDA JACOBSON

MARY KORMAN

MARILYN LYLE

MOIRA MACKIE

HELEN MILES

VAL ROBINSON

JOAN WILSON.

THE CALL GOES OUT - "THE BRIDGE CLUB IS COMING," AND THE FAMILY FEELS THE ICY GRIP OF APPREHENSION UNTIL RECIPE BOOKS ARE COMBED, THE PAGES BENT AND STICKY WITH PERSPIRATION, AND THE FINAL CHOICES ARE MADE. WOULD YOU RATHER SERVE EIGHT COMPANY PRESIDENTS?

THEN YOU SLOG THROUGH THE SUPERMARKET, RUNNY NOSED CHILDREN CLINGING TO YOUR SKIRTS, SEARCHING FOR SOME OBSCURE INGREDIENT THAT MAY ONLY BE PURCHASED BY THE POUND AND YOU ONLY NEED 1 TEASPOON.

AT 7:00 P.M. THE MOUSSE WON'T MOLD, AND YOU'RE STILL TRYING TO RIPEN THE AVOCADOS AFTER ALREADY TRYING VARIOUS METHODS TO SOFTEN (SETTLE FOR CANNED PEARS - POACHING, BAKING, HAMMERING, MASHING, GRATING OR ANY OTHER RECOURSE SIMPLY WILL <u>NOT</u> WORK TO REMOVE THAT PINE NEEDLE TASTE OR TEXTURE.) THE KIDS HAVE JUST LEFT A BATHTUB RING THAT NO COMMERCIAL CLEANSER COULD LIFT BEFORE A SOLID OVERNIGHT SOAKING, BUT THAT OPPORTUNITY HAS JUST AFFORDED ITSELF BECAUSE OF THE MISSING FACECLOTH. AND WHAT ELSE, THE KING IS VACATING THE PREMISES FASTER THAN A BOLT OF LIGHTNING FOR FEAR OF

BEING IDENTIFIED WITH SUCH A HOMEY ATMOSPHERE. THAT'S WHEN YOU KNOW FOR SURE – "THE BRIDGE CLUB IS COMING."

WELL, RELAX – HELP IS AT HAND. AFTER ELEVEN YEARS OF LAUGHTER AND TEARS, WE HAVE WRITTEN THIS BOOK TO SHARE WITH YOU OUR "BEST OF BRIDGE." WHO ELSE BUT THE LADIES FULLY APPRECIATE, OR EVEN NOTICE, THE FINER POINTS OF YOUR LATEST OFFERING FROM THE BOARD? OUR CLUB HAS REMAINED FAIRLY CONSTANT AND GENERALLY "SUB-FREE," TO WHICH WE ATTRIBUTE AN UNFAILING INTEREST IN FOOD. WE SERVE BOTH A MAIN DISH AND DESSERT, BUT FINALLY VOTED OUT CANDIES BY A NARROW MARGIN AFTER OUTSIDERS WOULD GASP AT THE FEAST LAID BEFORE THEM AT 11:00 P.M. MEMBERS ARRIVE ON TIME AND AN ATMOSPHERE OF "LET'S GET DOWN TO THE CARDS AND GET IT OVER WITH" PREVAILS. AFTER A MANDATORY THREE ROUNDS ANTICIPATION IS FEVER PITCHED, AS WE HEAR OUR HOSTESS CLATTERING IN THE KITCHEN, FROM WHICH ONLY THE BEST OF AROMAS EMANATE

THE IDEA FOR THIS BOOK WAS CONCEIVED ON OUR ANNUAL BRIDGE WORKSHOP HELD IN THE SPRING. WE PACK OUR BAGS, LEAVE DAD

WITH OUR DARLINGS ("DIAPERS ARE ON THE COUNTER, LOVE"), AND WE HEAD TO THE COTTAGE FOR TWO BOUNTIFUL DAYS OF BRIDGE, BACARDI'S AND BUFFETS.

DURING THE CHRISTMAS SEASON, EACH OF US BAKE EIGHT DOZEN OF OUR OWN FAVORITE GOODIES, WHICH WE EXCHANGE WITH EACH OTHER. IT PROVIDES A JOLLY BRIDGE NIGHT AND A GREAT WAY TO AMASS FESTIVE FARE.

THESE THREE AREAS, THEREFORE, ARE THE MAIN CONTENT OF THE FOLLOWING PAGES. SHOULD YOU FIND DIFFICULTY WITH ANY RECIPE, OR WISH TO OBTAIN MORE COPIES, PLEASE WRITE TO "THE BEST OF BRIDGE," 3029-3 ST. S.W. CALGARY, ALBERTA, T2S 1V2 WE WILL WELCOME ALL COMMENTS OR CRITICISMS, HOWEVER, WE WISH FOR YOU ONLY UNQUALIFIED SUCCESS AND, OF COURSE, "THE BEST OF BRIDGE."

RECIPE FOR THE BEST OF BRIDGE

8 "LADIES" PREFERABLY WHO HAVE
1. NO KILLER INSTINCT
2. NO CHILDREN OR DOGS
3. AN ABILITY TO COUNT TO 40
4. NOT EATEN DINNER

2 BOTTLES OR SO OF WINE
2 BRIDGE TABLES, WITH ASHTRAYS
1 'BOOK OF GOREN'
8 SENSES OF HUMOUR
1 GOOD LUNCH FROM 'THE BEST OF BRIDGE'

SET UP TABLES, POUR WINE, READ THE BENEDICTION FROM FATHER CHARLES AND PRAY FOR GOOD CARDS. POST 'RULES AND REGULATIONS' AS FOLLOWS:

NO MORE THAN 3 GLASSES OF WINE PER LADY
NO SNARLING
NO TRUMPING YOUR PARTNER'S ACE
NO TABLE TALK, SIGNALLING, FACIAL EXPRESSIONS OR "EXPLETIVES" (JUST ARRANGING) ALLOWED
TALK OF CHILDREN, DOGS OR LATEST OPERATION STRICTLY PROHIBITED.
NO CANDIES OR OTHER NIBBLIES.
NO DIETS ALLOWED.
NO HELPING WITH THE DISHES (YOUR TURN WILL COME)
DO HAVE A LAUGH.

PERK THE SANKA AND RELAX— YOUR LUNCH IS READY AND THE LADIES WILL RAVE.

PICTURED ON COVER:
CREPES WITH SEAFOOD OR CHICKEN FILLING
FOR RECIPE SEE PAGE 34

FLOWERS BY COLONIAL FLOWER SHOPPE, CALGARY.

I LUNCHEONS

NEW ORLEANS STRIPS

PERFECT FOR A COFFEE PARTY!

- 2 EGGS
- 1 TBSP. SUGAR
- FEW GRAINS SALT
- 3/4 CUPS MILK
- 1 TBSP. GRATED ORANGE RIND
- 12 THIN SLICES BREAD
- BUTTER

REMOVE CRUSTS FROM BREAD. BEAT EGGS, ADD SUGAR, SALT, MILK AND ORANGE RIND. DIP BREAD SLICES QUICKLY IN MILK MIXTURE AND FRY IN BUTTER UNTIL GOLDEN. SPRINKLE WITH ORANGE SUGAR AND SERVE IMMEDIATELY.

ORANGE SUGAR:

- 1/2 CUP SUGAR
- 1/4 CUP GRATED ORANGE PEEL

IF YOU WAIT TOO LONG TO MARRY YOUR DREAMBOAT, YOU MAY FIND, BY THE TIME YOU HAVE MADE UP YOUR MIND, HIS CARGO HAS SHIFTED.

SAVE YOUR 16 OZ. AND 48 OZ. FRUIT JUICE CANS TO USE AS MOLDS.

- 3 BEATEN EGGS
- ½ CUP COOKING OIL
- ½ CUP MILK
- 2½ CUPS SIFTED FLOUR
- 1 CUP SUGAR
- 1 TSP. BAKING POWDER
- 1 TSP. BAKING SODA
- 2 TSP. CINNAMON
- (1 TSP. EACH NUTMEG & GINGER - OPTIONAL)
- ½ TSP. SALT
- 2 CUPS SHREDDED CARROT
- 1½ CUPS COCONUT
- ½ CUP CHOPPED MARASCHINO CHERRIES (DRAINED)
- ½ CUP RAISINS
- ½ CUP CHOPPED PECANS

IN LARGE BOWL, SIFT TOGETHER DRY INGREDIENTS. COMBINE EGGS, OIL AND MILK, AND ADD TO FIRST MIXTURE. WHEN WELL-COMBINED, ADD ADDITIONAL INGREDIENTS. TURN INTO 4 - 16 OZ. CANS, LOAF PANS OR LARGE JUICE CANS. LINE GREASED CANS WITH WAXED PAPER. BAKE AT 350° FOR 50 TO 60 MINUTES. REMOVE FROM CANS AND COOL. THIS MAY BE KEPT IN REFRIGERATOR FOR SEVERAL WEEKS. SERVE BUTTERED SLICES AT BRUNCH INSTEAD OF TOAST.

OAT MUFFINS

- 1 CUP OATMEAL
- 1 CUP BUTTERMILK
- 1 CUP FLOUR
- 1 TSP. BAKING POWDER
- ½ TSP. BAKING SODA
- ½ TSP. SALT
- 1 BEATEN EGG
- 4 TBSPS. MELTED BUTTER
- ½ CUP RAISINS OR SNIPPED DATES
- RIND OF 1 ORANGE
- 1 CUP BROWN SUGAR

LET OATMEAL STAND FOR 10 MINUTES IN BUTTERMILK. COMBINE FLOUR, BAKING POWDER, SODA, SALT AND BROWN SUGAR. ADD EGG AND BUTTER, MIXING WELL. THEN POURING IN BUTTERMILK MIXTURE, ADD RAISINS AND PEEL. BAKE AT 400° FOR 20 MINUTES IN GREASED MUFFIN TINS.

DON'T BE TOO FUSSY, GIRLS. THERE ARE WOMEN WHO WAITED SO LONG FOR THEIR SHIP TO COME IN, THEIR PIER COLLAPSED.

2 PKGS. RAPID MIX YEAST
1/2 CUP SUGAR
2 TSPS. SALT
1/4 CUP MARGARINE
2 CUPS WATER
1 EGG, BEATEN
6 1/2 CUPS FLOUR

MIX 1/4 AMOUNT OF FLOUR WITH OTHER DRY INGREDIENTS. HEAT LIQUIDS UNTIL HOT TO TOUCH. ADD LIQUIDS TO DRY MIXTURE AND BEAT 2 MINUTES ON MEDIUM SPEED.

ADD 1/2 CUP FLOUR, BEATEN EGG. MIX ONE MINUTE. ADD FLOUR GRADUALLY (MAY NOT NEED ALL FLOUR.) FORM A BALL AND PUT IN GREASED BOWL. TURN OVER SO TOP IS GREASED. COVER WITH FOIL AND REFRIGERATE TWO HOURS.

TAKE 1/4 DOUGH AND SHAPE INTO BALLS - 1 INCH DIAMETER. PUT IN LIGHTLY GREASED 8" ROUND PAN. COVER AND LET RISE (35 MINUTES TO 45 MINUTES) COMBINE GARLIC SALT AND BUTTER AND MELT. BRUSH LIGHTLY ON TOP OF BALLS. SPRINKLE ON PARSLEY. COVER AND LET RISE ADDITIONAL 5 MINUTES. BAKE IN 400° OVEN FOR 15 MINUTES.

DOUGH MAY BE REFRIGERATED FOR TWO DAYS.

JIFFY ORANGE BREAD

2 CUPS FLOUR
1 TSP. BAKING POWDER
1 TSP. BAKING SODA
½ TSP. SALT
½ CUP CHOPPED NUTS
2 TBSPS. BUTTER
1 RIND OF ORANGE
  (GRATED)

⅓ CUP ORANGE JUICE
2 TSPS. VANILLA
1 CUP WHITE SUGAR
1 BEATEN EGG
½ CUP BOILING WATER

TOPPING:

1 TBSP. SUGAR
1 TBSP. ORANGE RIND
1 TBSP. CHOPPED NUTS

SIFT FLOUR, BAKING POWDER, SODA AND SALT. CREAM TOGETHER BUTTER, ORANGE PEEL, JUICE, VANILLA, SUGAR, BEATEN EGG AND BOILING WATER. ADD DRY INGREDIENTS BEATING JUST UNTIL FLOUR DISAPPEARS. TURN INTO GREASED LOAF PAN AND SPRINKLE WITH LAST THREE INGREDIENTS. BAKE AT 350° FOR 30 TO 40 MINUTES, OR UNTIL IT TESTS DONE.

MOTHERS ARE THOSE WONDERFUL PEOPLE WHO CAN GET UP IN THE MORNING BEFORE THEY SMELL THE BACON FRYING.

GARLIC-PARMESAN CHEESE BREAD

1 CUP MILK
¼ LB. BUTTER
1 TBSP. PAPRIKA
GARLIC TO TASTE

HEAT ALL INGREDIENTS TOGETHER. DIP FRENCH BREAD SLICES IN QUICKLY, COVERING BOTH SIDES. ROLL UNTIL COMPLETELY COVERED IN PARMESAN CHEESE. BAKE AT 400° FOR 5 MINUTES. WATCH THEM CAREFULLY SO THEY DON'T BURN. THE FRENCH BREAD SLICES MAY BE HALVED SO WHEN THEY ARE DIPPED THEY DON'T GET TOO SOGGY. USE A SHALLOW PAN FOR THE DIPPING.

TWO PEOPLE CAN LIVE AS CHEAPLY AS ONE WHAT?

HERB BREAD

1 LOAF FRENCH BREAD
½ CUP SOFT BUTTER
2 TSPS. GARLIC POWDER
½ TSP. SAVORY
1 TSP. CELERY SALT
½ TSP. ROSEMARY
½ TSP. THYME
½ TSP. CHERVIL
½ TSP. BASIL
1 TSP. SAGE
3 TSP. PARSLEY
½ TSP. OREGANO

COMBINE ALL INGREDIENTS. SPREAD ON SLICED BREAD. WRAP IN FOIL. HEAT IN 350° OVEN FOR 30 MINUTES.

PICTURED ON PAGE 17 ARE;
RENE'S SANDWICH LOAF - PAGE 30
POPPY-SEED SALAD DRESSING WITH
FRESH FRUIT SALAD - PAGE 119
BRANDY MINT CREAM - PAGE 60

FLOWERS BY COLONIAL FLOWER SHOPPE, CALGARY.

GOURMET TOAST

A GOOD LATE-NIGHT SNACK. COMBINE ALL INGREDIENTS EXCEPT FOR WINE-REFRIGERATE UNTIL READY TO BAKE.

- 1 SLICE FRENCH BREAD
- 4 VERY THIN SLICES DILL PICKLE
- 4 VERY THIN SLICES TOMATO
- 1 SLICE HAM
- 1 SLICE SWISS CHEESE
- 1 OZ. DRY WHITE WINE
- FRESHLY GROUND BLACK PEPPER
- 2 TBSPS. BUTTER

PAN-FRY BOTH SIDES OF BREAD IN THE BUTTER TO A GOLDEN BROWN. PLACE IN A BAKING DISH OR PAN. COVER FIRST WITH PICKLES, THEN TOMATOES, HAM AND FINALLY CHEESE. POUR WINE OVER THE WHOLE THING, AND BAKE OR BROIL UNTIL THE CHEESE MELTS EVENLY. GRIND BLACK PEPPER OVER THE TOP TO TASTE.

DOCTORS WILL TELL YOU THAT IF YOU EAT SLOWLY, YOU WILL EAT LESS. THAT IS PARTICULARLY TRUE IF YOU ARE A MEMBER OF A LARGE FAMILY.

½ LB. CUBED HAM
½ LB. CUBED CHEDDAR CHEESE
3 TSP. SLICED GREEN OLIVES
½ CUP EACH, CHILI SAUCE
    AND MAYONNAISE

MIX INGREDIENTS AND FILL BUNS. BAKE AT 400° FOR 15 MINUTES. CHILI RECIPE BELOW:

CHILI SAUCE

1 28 OZ. TIN TOMATOES
1 CUP BROWN SUGAR
1 CUP VINEGAR
1 LARGE CHOPPED ONION
1 TSP. CINNAMON
1 TSP. ALLSPICE
SPRINKLE OF GINGER
CHILI PEPPERS

THESE INGREDIENTS ARE COOKED TOGETHER UNTIL THE MIXTURE THICKENS AND BECOMES A DARK RED. THIS WILL TAKE PRETTY WELL THE WHOLE DAY AT LOW HEAT. STIR OCCASIONALLY. THE TOMATOES SHOULD BE CUT UP. USE YOUR DISCRETION WITH THE CHILI PEPPERS. USE THE BOTTLED CRUSHED CHILIES FROM THE SPICE SECTION. I KEEP TASTING IT THROUGH THE DAY AND ADD MORE UNTIL IT IS AS HOT AS I WANT IT. THIS IS A NICE CONDIMENT WITH BEEF OR MACARONI DISH.

CRAB AND DEVILED EGG SANDWICH

1 CAN CRAB MEAT
2 HARD BOILED EGGS
½ TSP. MUSTARD (PREPARED)
2 TBSPS. MAYONNAISE
1 TBSP. LEMON JUICE
½ SMALL TSP. CURRY POWDER

DRAIN CRAB MEAT. MIX WITH OTHER INGREDIENTS. LOBSTER OR CHICKEN MAY BE USED. SERVE IN SMALL BUNS.

WHEN A MAN BRINGS HOME FLOWERS FOR NO REASON, THERE'S A REASON.

CRAB AND CHEESE TOASTIES

1 CAN CRAB MEAT
2 TBSPS. BUTTER OR MARGARINE
1 8 OZ. PACKAGE PROCESSED CHEESE
4 HAMBURGER BUNS

FLAKE CRAB MEAT MELT BUTTER AND CHEESE OVER LOW HEAT; STIRRING UNTIL SMOOTH. ADD CRAB MEAT. CUT BUNS IN HALF AND SPREAD WITH CRAB MIXTURE. PLACE UNDER BROILER FOR 3 MINUTES UNTIL SLIGHTLY BROWN AND BUBBLY.

FAST SHRIMP ROLLS

1 PKG. CREAM CHEESE
1 TBSP. MILK
2 TSP. LEMON JUICE
1 TBSP. CHOPPED GREEN ONION
½ TSP. WORCESTERSHIRE SAUCE
SALT AND PEPPER
3 TO 5 LONG CRUSTY ROLLS
CANNED OR COOKED SHRIMP
CHOPPED PARSLEY

MIX CHEESE, MILK AND LEMON JUICE, BLEND UNTIL SMOOTH. ADD ONION, WORCESTERSHIRE SAUCE, SALT AND PEPPER; MIX WELL. CUT ROLLS LENGTHWISE. HEAT ROLLS IN FOIL IN OVEN. SPREAD WITH CHEESE MIXTURE. PLACE SHRIMP ON TOP AND SPRINKLE WITH PARSLEY.

IT'S SO EASY TO TELL A MARRIED COUPLE THESE DAYS. THE HUSBAND IS THE ONE WHO ENTERS THE CAR FROM THE LEFT OR STREET SIDE. THE WIFE IS THE ONE WHO CLIMBS OVER THE SNOWBANK ON THE RIGHT SIDE.

BRIDGE PIZZAS

RYE BREAD (TOAST EACH SLICE LIGHTLY)
1 SMALL TIN TOMATO PASTE
1/4 TSP. GARLIC SALT
1/4 TSP. ONION SALT
1 OREGANO LEAF, CRUSHED

MIX TOGETHER TOMATO PASTE, GARLIC SALT, ONION SALT AND OREGANO LEAF AND SPREAD ON RYE BREAD. PUT SLICE OF MOZZARELLA CHEESE AND PARMESAN ON PASTE. PUT ON ANY PIZZA INGREDIENTS YOU LIKE; MUSHROOMS, CHERRY TOMATO SLICES, ONION, PEPPERONI, SALAMI, GREEN PEPPER.

COVER WITH LARGE SLICE OF MOZZARELLA CHEESE AND BROIL TILL CHEESE MELTS AND IS BUBBLY HOT.

SEAFOOD SALAD SANDWICHES

1 CAN SMALL SHRIMP
1 CAN CRAB MEAT
1 PKG. PHILADELPHIA CREAM CHEESE

SOFTEN CHEESE AND ADD SEAFOOD. SPREAD ON WARM HOLLAND RUSKS. TOP WITH SLICE OF TOMATO AND CHEDDAR CHEESE. HEAT IN MODERATE OVEN UNTIL CHEESE IS MELTED (15 TO 20 MINUTES.)

TACOS (MEXICAN HAMBURGERS)

1 PKG. LAWRY'S TACO SHELLS
1 PKG. LAWRY'S TACO SEASONING
1 LB. GROUND BEEF

BROWN GROUND BEEF, ADD SEASONING AND WATER. SIMMER 15 TO 20 MINUTES.

PREPARE AND PUT INTO INDIVIDUAL BOWLS:

CHOPPED TOMATOES
SHREDDED LETTUCE
SHREDDED CHEDDAR CHEESE
CHOPPED OLIVES
CHOPPED GREEN ONIONS
SOUR CREAM (HELPS HOLD TOGETHER)
MAYONNAISE
AVOCADO

FILL TACO SHELLS WITH MEAT MIXTURE AND ADD ANY OR ALL OF THE ABOVE.

EVER NOTICE THAT THE JOLLY GREEN GIANT STANDS AROUND LAUGHING HIS HEAD OFF WHILE THE LITTLE PEOPLE DO ALL THE WORK CANNING VEGETABLES.

HAM CHEESE TOWERS

RAISIN BREAD
SHAVED HAM
MILD CHEESE SLICES

TRIM EACH SLICE OF BREAD TO REMOVE CRUSTS. (SCISSORS ARE OFTEN FASTEST METHOD, IF BREAD IS REALLY FRESH, AND THE WASTE IS NOT EXCESSIVE.) EACH SANDWICH REQUIRES THREE SLICES OF BREAD. BUTTER EACH SLICE AND PILE A GENEROUS PORTION OF HAM ON TWO SLICES OF BREAD TOPPING WITH THIRD SLICE. TOP WITH A SLICE OF CHEESE. THESE MAY BE MADE AHEAD AND FROZEN ON COOKIE SHEET. REMOVE FROM FREEZER SEVERAL HOURS AHEAD OF SERVING TIME. ONE HALF HOUR BEFORE SERVING, PLACE IN 250° OVEN, COVERED, REMOVING FOIL DURING LAST 3 MINUTES, AND TURNING OVEN TO 'BROIL.' WATCH CAREFULLY NOT TO BURN. SERVE WITH PICKLES. THESE ARE FILLING AND DELICIOUS.

IF YOU WANT TO GET SOMETHING FOR YOUR MONEY, BUY A PURSE.

COCKTAIL SANDWICHES

Make a tray of individual fancy sandwiches - great as you can do this a day before.

SUGGESTIONS:

Chopped egg and onion

Meat - ham, chicken, beef

Peanut butter and banana (rolled)

Cheese and pickle (rolled)

Asparagus and cream cheese (rolled)

Crab, lobster or shrimp

Girls who think they will hate themselves in the morning should sleep till noon.

CRAB AND CHEESE BUNS

2/3	lb. Velveeta cheese
2/3	lb. butter
2	cans crab
18	Parker House rolls

Have cheese and butter at room temperature and then whip together. Add crab and fill buns really full. Put in oven at 325° until warm and cheese has melted.

REUBEN SANDWICHES

PREPARE THESE AHEAD OF TIME—
EITHER FREEZE OR REFRIGERATE UNTIL
TIME TO GRILL.

THIN SLICED RYE BREAD
(2 PER SANDWICH)
THOUSAND ISLAND DRESSING
SWISS CHEESE SLICES
1 TBSP. DRAINED SAUERKRAUT
PER SANDWICH
12 PAPER-THIN SLICES CORNED BEEF
PER SANDWICH

SPREAD THOUSAND ISLAND DRESSING ON
BOTTOM SLICES OF RYE BREAD, TOP WITH
1 TO 2 SLICES OF CHEESE, 1 TBSP. SAUERKRAUT;
MOUND CORNED BEEF AND TOP WITH SECOND
SLICE OF BREAD. BUTTER OUTSIDE, TOP AND
BOTTOM. COVER AND REFRIGERATE UNTIL
READY TO GRILL. MELT BUTTER IN HEAVY
SKILLET THEN GRILL UNTIL BROWNED AND
CHEESE IS MELTED.

THERE IS ONE ADVANTAGE IN BEING
MARRIED. YOU CAN'T MAKE A FOOL OF
YOURSELF WITHOUT KNOWING IT.

DON'T FORGET THE SIMPLE PLEASURES OF FRESH BREAD AND COOL ASPARAGUS. A DELICIOUS DELIGHT AND A FAVORITE OF WOMEN AND MEN ALIKE - EASY ON THE HOSTESS TOO - A MAKE-AHEAD.

2 CANS GREEN ASPARAGUS
2 SANDWICH LOAVES
MAYONNAISE, SALT, SEASONED PEPPER
BUTTER.

DRAIN ASPARAGUS IN CAN FOR A FEW MINUTES, THEN SPREAD OUT ON PAPER TOWELS, TO ALLOW IT TO BE COMPLETELY DRAINED AND DRY, 2 HOURS BEFORE MAKING SANDWICHES. TRIM CRUSTS FROM BREAD, BUTTER SLICES THEN SPREAD GENEROUSLY WITH MAYONNAISE. PLACE AN ASPARAGUS SPEAR AT ONE END OF PIECE OF BREAD, SPRINKLE WITH SALT AND PEPPER AND ROLL UP. PLACE ON SERVING PLATE. COVER WITH FOIL AND REFRIGERATE UNTIL ½ HOUR BEFORE SERVING. MAKES ABOUT 40 SMALL SANDWICHES.

(SEE PICTURE) PAGE 141.

EARLY TO BED AND EARLY TO RISE MEANS A MAN GETS HIS OWN BREAKFAST.

HAM 'N CHEESE PARTY SANDWICH

    RAISIN BREAD
    HAM SLICES
    PHILADELPHIA CREAM CHEESE

SOFTEN CHEESE WITH MILK AND A SMALL AMOUNT OF MAYONNAISE SO THAT IT'S EASY TO SPREAD.

FOR EACH INDIVIDUAL SANDWICH YOU NEED TWO SLICES OF BREAD. ON THE OUTSIDE OF EACH SLICE SPREAD CHEESE MIXTURE. BUTTER INSIDE AND FILL WITH TWO SLICES OF HAM. TOP EACH SANDWICH WITH A CURLED CARROT ON A TOOTH PICK.

YOU MAY SERVE THESE SANDWICHES COLD OR STICK UNDER BROILER UNTIL CHEESE BUBBLES. SERVE WITH A PICKLE TRAY AND BEVERAGE.

HAPPINESS IS GETTING UP AT 3:00 A.M. TO FEED THE BABY AND FINDING TWO BOTTLES.... ONE FOR THE BABY, AND ONE FOR YOU.

RENE'S SANDWICH LOAF

UNSLICED SANDWICH LOAF
2   3 OZ. PKG. CREAM CHEESE
        (SOFTENED WITH MILK)

HAM FILLING:
    1   CUP GROUND COOKED HAM
    2   TBSPS. PICKLE RELISH, DRAINED
    ½   TSP. HORSE RADISH
    ⅓   CUP FINELY CHOPPED CELERY
    ¼   CUP MAYONNAISE

ASPARAGUS TIP FILLING:
    1   CAN ASPARAGUS TIPS, DRAINED
    CHEESE WHIZ

EGG FILLING:
    4   HARD BOILED EGGS, CHOPPED
    2   TBSPS. FINELY CHOPPED GREEN ONIONS
    ½   TSP. PREPARED MUSTARD
    ¼   CUP MAYONNAISE
    SALT AND PEPPER TO TASTE.

TRIM CRUSTS FROM SANDWICH LOAF-SLICE
BREAD LENGTHWISE IN FOUR EQUAL LAYERS.
BUTTER EACH SLICE. SPREAD FIRST LAYER
WITH HAM FILLING, SECOND LAYER WITH
ASPARAGUS TIP FILLING AND THIRD LAYER
WITH EGG FILLING. BEAT CREAM CHEESE
WITH MILK TILL FLUFFY. FROST TOP AND SIDES OF
LOAF. SPRINKLE GENEROUSLY WITH CHOPPED
PARSLEY OR SLICED STUFFED OLIVES. CONTINUED!

SANDWICH LOAF

CONTINUED!

WRAP THE LOAF LOOSELY IN FOIL AND STORE IN REFRIGERATOR TILL SERVING TIME. STRICTLY FOR COMPANY AND SIMPLY DELICIOUS. SERVES 8 TO 10. (SEE PICTURE PAGE 17)

ONE OF THE FIRST THINGS A GAL LEARNS AFTER MARRIAGE IS THAT CANDY COMES IN 15¢ BARS, AS WELL AS $5.00 BOXES.

GRILLED CHEESE ITALIANO

FOR EACH SANDWICH:
2 SLICES RYE BREAD
1 SLICE MOZZARELLA CHEESE
1 OR 2 SLICES OF SALAMI

GENEROUSLY BUTTER TOP AND BOTTOM OF SLICES OF RYE BREAD. GRILL ON BOTH SIDES UNTIL GOLDEN BROWN.

SERVE WITH DILL PICKLES AND ONION.

31

HAM BUNS

MINCE ONE POUND OF HAM. (FREEZE YOUR LEFTOVER READY TO EAT HAM TO USE FOR ENTERTAINING EMERGENCIES.)

TO MINCED HAM, ADD THE FOLLOWING;

- 3 TO 4 STALKS FINELY CHOPPED CELERY
- 1 SMALL ONION, CHOPPED FINE
- 1/2 CUP MAYONNAISE
- 2 TSP. MUSTARD
- 1/2 TSP. WORCESTERSHIRE SAUCE
- SPRINKLE WITH LAWRY SEASONED SALT

MIX ALL INGREDIENTS WELL, TO MOISTEN THOROUGHLY. SPLIT PARKER HOUSE ROLLS, BUTTER, AND PILE IN FILLING. THESE CAN BE PREPARED DAYS BEFORE, WRAPPED IN FOIL AND FROZEN UNTIL NEEDED. TO SERVE, HEAT IN 350° OVEN, COVERED IN FOIL UNTIL WARMED THROUGH, ABOUT 1/2 AN HOUR.

PEOPLE GO ON VACATIONS TO FORGET THINGS AND WHEN THEY OPEN THEIR BAGS, THEY FIND OUT THEY DID.

Hot Tuna Pizza Burgers

⅓ cup Mayonnaise
½ tsp. salt
¼ tsp. oregano
1 tbsp. grated or minced onion
¼ cup tomato paste
¼ cup water
Grated parmesan cheese
1 7oz. can solid tuna-drained
   and broken up
4 hamburger buns, split

Blend together mayonnaise, salt, tuna, onion, oregano. Spread on bun halves. Blend tomato paste and water. Spoon over tuna mixture. Sprinkle with grated parmesan cheese using 1 or 2 tsp. on each. Place in 400° oven. Bake 10 minutes. Serve immediately.

Woman is nothing but a rag, a bone and a hank of hair. Man is nothing but a brag, a groan and a tank of air.

OPEN FACE HAM BUNS

½ LB. VELVEETA CHEESE (CUBED)
½ LB. COOKED HAM (CUBED)
2 HARD BOILED EGGS (CHOPPED)
½ CUP GREEN OLIVES (SLICED)
⅓ CUP CHOPPED ONIONS
2 TBSPS. MIRACLE WHIP
½ CUP CHILI SAUCE
1 DOZ. HAMBURGER BUNS (SPLIT)

COMBINE ALL INGREDIENTS. SPREAD ON BUN HALVES. PLACE UNDER BROILER 5 TO 8 MINUTES OR UNTIL MIXTURE IS BUBBLY AND CHEESE IS MELTED. SERVE HOT. MAKES ENOUGH FOR 2 DOZEN BUN HALVES.

CHICKEN OR CRAB CRÊPES

BATTER:

1 CUP COLD WATER
1 CUP COLD MILK
4 EGGS
½ TSP. SALT
2 CUPS FLOUR
2 TBSPS. MELTED BUTTER

PUT ALL INGREDIENTS IN BLENDER JAR, COVER AND BLEND 2 MINUTES. REFRIGERATE 2 HOURS. USING 6 INCH CRÊPE PAN, MAKE CRÊPES AS THIN AS POSSIBLE. (CONT'D NEXT PAGE.

PICTURED ON PAGE 35 ;

SEAFOOD SCALLOP SHELLS. PAGE 39

FILLING:

- 4 TBSPS. CHOPPED GREEN ONION
- 4 TBSPS. BUTTER
- ½ CUP SHERRY
- 3 CUPS DICED CRAB OR CHICKEN
- SALT AND PEPPER

SAUTÉ ONION IN BUTTER - ADD SHERRY AND MIX WITH CRAB. SET ASIDE FOR SAUCE.

SAUCE:

- 4 TBSPS. BUTTER
- 5 TBSPS. FLOUR
- 2 CUPS HOT MILK
- SALT AND PEPPER
- 2 EGG YOLKS
- ½ CUP HEAVY CREAM
- ¾ CUP SWISS CHEESE (GRATED)

MELT BUTTER AND ADD FLOUR AND BLEND. ADD MILK, SEASONING, BOIL FOR 1 MINUTE AND REMOVE FROM HEAT. BEAT YOLKS AND CREAM. ADD YOLKS - STIRRING CONSTANTLY. FOLD IN CHEESE, SHOULD BE THICK. ADD SAUCE TO FILLING. RESERVE ENOUGH TO POUR OVER CRÊPES. IF TOO THICK YOU MAY THIN THIS OUT WITH CREAM. PICTURED ON COVER.

CRABMEAT QUICHE

PREHEAT OVEN TO 375°

MAKE A 9" PASTRY SHELL

2 TBSPS. GREEN ONIONS

3 TBSPS. BUTTER

1 CUP CRAB MEAT (OR SHRIMP)

2 TBSPS. MADEIRA OR DRY
                WHITE VERMOUTH

3 EGGS

1 CUP WHIPPING CREAM

1 TBSP. TOMATO PASTE

SALT AND PEPPER TO TASTE

¼ CUP GRATED CHEDDAR CHEESE

SAUTÉ ONIONS IN BUTTER. BEAT EGGS AND CREAM, ADD TOMATO PASTE, SALT AND PEPPER. ADD CRABMEAT AND MADEIRA TO ONIONS. BOIL FOR A MINUTE SO WINE EVAPORATES. PUT FISH MIXTURE INTO EGGS AND CREAM MIXTURE. BAKE PASTRY SHELL AND PARTIALLY COOK IT. COOL. ADD FILLING. SPRINKLE WITH ¼ CUP GRATED CHEDDAR CHEESE. BAKE 30 MINUTES UNTIL FIRM.

MARRIED LIFE IS LIKE SITTING IN THE BATHTUB.... AFTER AWHILE, IT'S NOT SO HOT.

SEAFOOD SCALLOP SHELLS
(SEE PICTURE)

A PERFECT MAKE AHEAD. ALL INGREDIENTS CAN BE COMBINED, PLACED IN SHELLS AND FROZEN WITHOUT COOKING. JUST THAW AND BAKE TO SERVE.

- 1 10 OZ. CAN CREAM OF CELERY SOUP
- ¼ CUP MILK
- 1 BEATEN EGG
- ¼ CUP PARMESAN CHEESE
- 1 5 OZ. CAN CRAB MEAT, FLAKED
- 1 4¼ OZ. CAN SHRIMP, RINSED & DRAINED
- 1 10 OZ. CAN SLICED MUSHROOMS, DRAINED
- ¼ CUP FINE BREAD CRUMBS
- 1 TBSP. MELTED BUTTER

COMBINE SOUP, MILK, BEATEN EGG AND 2 TBSPS. CHEESE IN SAUCEPAN. STIR OVER LOW HEAT TILL HOT. ADD SEAFOOD AND MUSHROOMS. SPOON INTO ONE LARGE CASSEROLE OR FOUR LARGE SHELLS.

MELT BUTTER. ADD LAST 2 TBSPS. CHEESE AND BREAD CRUMBS. SPRINKLE OVER SEAFOOD MIXTURE. BAKE AT 375° FOR 30 MINUTES.

THIS RECIPE MAY BE DOUBLED.

THIS IS GREAT FOR AN AFTER FOOTBALL GATHERING SERVED WITH A SALAD.

- 2 TBSPS. CHOPPED GREEN ONION
- 2 TBSPS. BUTTER
- 1 CAN CRAB (LARGE TIN)
- 1 6 OZ. PKG. FROZEN COOKED SHRIMP
- 1/4 TSP. SALT
- 1/4 TSP. PEPPER
- 3 EGGS
- 1 CUP WHIPPING CREAM
- 1 OR 2 TBSP. CATSUP
- 1/4 TSP. SALT
- 9" PARTIALLY COOKED PASTRY SHELL
- 1/4 CUP GRATED SWISS CHEESE

PREHEAT OVEN TO 370° ^WHAT? COOK ONIONS IN BUTTER. ADD SHRIMP AND CRAB - STIR 2 MINUTES. SPRINKLE WITH SALT AND PEPPER. ALLOW TO COOL. BEAT EGGS WITH CREAM, CATSUP AND SALT. SLOWLY ADD SHRIMP AND CRAB. POUR INTO PASTRY SHELL AND SPRINKLE WITH CHEESE. BAKE IN UPPER PART OF OVEN FOR 25 TO 35 MINUTES UNTIL QUICHE IS PUFFED AND BROWNED.

SERVES 6 TO 8, PREHEAT OVEN TO 350°

- 1 CUP UNCOOKED RICE
- 2 PKGS. (6 OZ) FROZEN KING CRAB MEAT (THAWED)
- 2 TBSPS. BUTTER
- ½ CUP SLICES CELERY
- 1 CAN CONDENSED CREAM OF MUSHROOM SOUP
- 1 CUP SHREDDED CHEDDAR CHEESE
- 1 CUP PLAIN YOGURT
- ½ CUP CHOPPED GREEN PEPPER
- ¼ CUP CHOPPED ONION
- ¼ CUP CHOPPED PIMENTO
- ⅛ TSP. WORCESTERSHIRE SAUCE
- ½ TSP. SALT

COOK RICE ACCORDING TO PKG. DIRECTIONS. DRAIN CRAB MEAT — FLAKE. MELT BUTTER IN LARGE SKILLET. SAUTÉ CELERY, GREEN PEPPER AND ONION. REMOVE FROM HEAT; STIR IN SOUP, CHEESE, YOGURT, PIMENTO, SALT AND WORCESTERSHIRE SAUCE. LAYER RICE AND CRAB IN BAKING DISH AND POUR SAUCE OVER ALL. BAKE FOR 30 MINUTES.

BAKED CRAB CASSEROLE

½ CUP CURRANTS
½ CUP CHOPPED APPLE PEELED
   (ONE APPLE)
1 LB. CRAB MEAT
2 TBSP. FLOUR
1 CUP MILK
1 CUP CELERY (CHOPPED FINE)
3 CUPS HOT COOKED RICE
⅓ CUP BUTTER
CURRY POWDER- ADD AS DESIRED
SALT AND PEPPER TO TASTE
½ CUP CRUSHED CANNED ONION RINGS
   (FRIED)

COOK CURRANTS, CELERY AND APPLE IN SMALL AMOUNT OF WATER UNTIL SOFT. MAKE SAUCE WITH FLOUR, BUTTER AND CURRY POWDER, MELTING BUTTER AND ADDING FLOUR AND THE AMOUNT OF CURRY POWDER DESIRED. ADD MILK STIRRING CONSTANTLY. WHEN THICKENED ADD CURRANTS, CELERY AND APPLE. SALT AND PEPPER TO TASTE. PLACE COOKED RICE IN BUTTERED CASSEROLE. MIX CRAB MEAT WITH SAUCE MIXTURE. POUR OVER RICE. TOP WITH CRUSHED ONIONS. PLACE IN 375° OVEN AND COOK 25 MINUTES. SERVES 6.

CHEESE FONDUE

SERVES SIX.

- 2 CUPS DRY WHITE WINE
- ½ LB. SWISS EMMENTHAL CHEESE GRATED
- ½ LB. NATURAL GRUYÈRE - GRATED
- 2 TBSPS. FLOUR
- 1 CLOVE GARLIC, HALVED
- 3 TBSPS. BRANDY (OR MORE)
- FRENCH BREAD CUT IN CUBES
- SPRINKLE OF PAPRIKA

TOSS CHEESE WITH FLOUR IN LARGE BOWL. RUB CUT ENDS OF GARLIC AROUND 'CROCKERY FONDUE' DISH. POUR WINE IN FONDUE DISH AND HEAT SLOWLY OVER BURNER UNTIL BUBBLES RISE. STIR IN CHEESE MIXTURE (A SMALL AMOUNT AT A TIME) WITH WOODEN SPOON. LET EACH ADDITION MELT BEFORE ADDING MORE. STIR IN BRANDY AND SPRINKLE WITH PAPRIKA.

USE AS DIP FOR FRENCH BREAD.

IF YOU HAVE HALF A MIND TO GET MARRIED, DO IT! THAT'S ALL IT TAKES.

AVOCADO CRAB QUICKIE

THIS IS A FAST AND REFRESHING LUNCHEON MEAL.

- 4 RIPE AVOCADOS
- 2 LARGE CANS CRAB MEAT
- LETTUCE
- ½ CUP MAYONNAISE (OR TO TASTE)

SLICE AVOCADOS IN HALF, LENGTHWISE. (CUT AROUND AVOCADO THEN HOLD IN BOTH HANDS AND TWIST IN OPPOSITE DIRECTIONS TO SEPARATE.) REMOVE PIT. FLAKE CRAB MEAT, MIX IN MAYONNAISE. PLACE MIXTURE IN AVOCADO HALVES AND SERVE ON A BED ON LETTUCE. SERVE WITH HOT ROLLS.

EVERY MAN SHOULD SERVE A HITCH IN THE SERVICE. HE LEARNS TO MAKE BEDS, TO TAKE ORDERS, NOT TO VOLUNTEER AND MANY OTHER SKILLS HE'LL NEED WHEN HE'S MARRIED.

SENATE SALAD BOWL

- 1 CUP TORN ICEBURG LETTUCE LEAVES
- 1 CUP TORN ROMAINE LETTUCE
- ½ CUP WATERCRESS, STEMS REMOVED
- 1 CUP DICED CELERY
- ¼ CUP CHOPPED GREEN ONION
- 1½ CUPS CUBED, COOKED LOBSTER
  OR SHRIMP
- 2 MEDIUM TOMATOES, DICED
- 1 AVOCADO, PEELED AND SLICED
- ½ MEDIUM GRAPEFRUIT, SECTIONED
- 5 LARGE PITTED RIPE OLIVES, SLICED
- ¼ CUP LEMON JUICE, FRESH,
  FROZEN OR CANNED.

CREAM DRESSING:

- 1 CUP CREAMED COTTAGE CHEESE
- ¼ TSP. SALT
- ¼ CUP SOUR CREAM
- DASH OF PEPPER

TOSS TOGETHER FIRST 5 INGREDIENTS IN LARGE SALAD BOWL. COMBINE NEXT 5 INGREDIENTS, SPRINKLE ALL WITH LEMON JUICE AND ADD TO GREENS. GARNISH WITH ADDITIONAL TOMATO SLICES AND RIPE OLIVES. REFRIGERATE UNTIL WELL CHILLED. MEANWHILE MAKE DRESSING, COMBINE ALL INGREDIENTS IN BLENDER OR MIXING BOWL AND BEAT UNTIL CREAMY SMOOTH. POUR OVER SALAD JUST BEFORE SERVING.

MEXICAN CHEF SALAD

1	LB. GROUND BEEF
1	15 OZ. CAN RED KIDNEY BEANS (DRAINED)
1	SMALL BUNCH GREEN ONIONS
1	HEAD OF LETTUCE
4	TOMATOES
1/4	LB. GRATED CHEDDAR CHEESE
8	OZ. THOUSAND ISLAND DRESSING OR FRENCH DRESSING
1	MEDIUM SIZE BAG TORTILLA CHIPS, CRUSHED
1	LARGE AVOCADO, DICED

BROWN GROUND BEEF, DRAIN, AND ADD KIDNEY BEANS, COOKING FOR 5 MINUTES. ALLOW TO COOL. CHOP LETTUCE, ONION, TOMATOES AND SALAD DRESSING. MIX BEEF AND BEANS INTO COLD SALAD INGREDIENTS ADD CRUSHED CHIPS. GARNISH WITH AVOCADO AND TOMATO WEDGES. SERVE IMMEDIATELY. IF MAKING AHEAD, RESERVE TORTILLA CHIPS AND ADD JUST BEFORE SERVING.

WHEN A MAN PUTS HIS FOOT DOWN, IT MEANS HIS WIFE HAS FINISHED VACUUMING UNDER THE CHAIR.

SHRIMP BOATS

- ¼ CUP VINEGAR
- 1 TBSP. CATSUP
- 2 TBSPS. HORSERADISH MUSTARD
- ½ TSP. TARRAGON
- 1½ TSPS. PAPRIKA
- ½ TSP. SALT
- ¼ TSP. CAYENNE
- ½ CUP SALAD OIL
- ¼ CUP FINELY CHOPPED CELERY
- ¼ CUP FINELY CHOPPED GREEN ONION
- 2 LBS. MEDIUM OR LARGE CLEANED, COOKED SHRIMP
- 4 RIPE AVOCADOS

COMBINE FIRST SEVEN INGREDIENTS, ADDING OIL SLOWLY AND BEATING CONSTANTLY. ADD CELERY AND ONIONS. POUR OVER THE SHRIMP AND REFRIGERATE 4 HOURS OR OVERNIGHT. HALVE AND PEEL AVOCADO AND ARRANGE SHRIMP ON EACH HALF. SERVE ON LETTUCE LEAVES WITH CHILLED ASPARAGUS, CARROT CURLS, SLICED BOILED EGGS, ALONG WITH MARINADE OR FRENCH DRESSING.

LOBSTER MOUSSE

THIS SALAD LOOKS PARTICULARLY ATTRACTIVE WHEN SERVED IN A FISH-SHAPED MOLD. THE CONTOURS OF THE FISH LEND THEMSELVES BEAUTIFULLY TO DECORATION. (PIMENTO AND GREEN PEPPER STRIPS FOR FINS AND GILLS AND SLICED STUFFED OLIVE FOR THE EYE.) SERVES 8 TO 10 PEOPLE.

2 PKGS. LEMON JELLO
1 CUP COLD WATER
1 CUP MIRACLE WHIP
2 TINS LOBSTER
½ CUP SLICED STUFFED OLIVES
3 TBSPS. CHOPPED PIMENTOS
1 TSP. GRATED ONION
2 CUPS HOT WATER
½ TSP. SALT
1½ CUPS DICED CELERY
4 TBSPS LEMON JUICE

DISSOLVE JELLO IN HOT WATER, ADD COLD WATER, LEMON JUICE, MIRACLE WHIP, SALT AND ONION. BLEND WITH ROTARY BEATER. POUR INTO BOWL AND REFRIGERATE UNTIL PARTIALLY JELLED (ABOUT ½ HOUR). OIL SALAD MOLD. CONTINUED NEXT PAGE!

A MAN'S HOME IS HIS HASSLE.

CONTINUED!

DECORATE BOTTOM OF MOLD WHILE WAITING, USING PIMENTO STRIPS, GREEN PEPPER STRIPS, SLICED STUFFED OLIVES. REMOVE GELATIN MIXTURE FROM FRIDGE AND WHIP UNTIL FLUFFY. FOLD IN REMAINING INGREDIENTS. POUR INTO DECORATED MOLD AND CHILL.

DECORATE WITH ENDIVE AND CHERRY TOMATOES.

SHRIMP SALAD

- 1 CUP COOKED RICE (AMOUNT MAY BE VARIED)
- 1 CUP MEDIUM COOKED SHRIMP, CLEANED AND PEELED.
- ¾ TSP. SALT
- 1 TBSP. LEMON JUICE
- 1 CUP DICED RAW CAULIFLOWER
- 1 TBSP. GREEN ONION
- 1 TBSP. CHOPPED GREEN OLIVES
- ½ CUP GREEN PEPPER
- 2 TBSPS. FRENCH DRESSING
- ¾ CUP MAYONNAISE

MIX ALL INGREDIENTS. SERVE ON LETTUCE LINED INDIVIDUAL SERVING PLATES GARNISHED WITH GREEN OLIVES AND TWO OR THREE EXTRA SHRIMP.

CURRIED CHICKEN BOATS

4   CHICKEN BREASTS (3 LBS.)
1   MEDIUM ONION, SLICED
1   STALK CELERY, CUT IN 1" PIECES
2½   TSPS. SALT.
6   WHOLE BLACK PEPPER CORNS
1   BAY LEAF
1   CUP MAYONNAISE
½   CUP HEAVY CREAM
¼   CUP CHUTNEY
½   TBSP. CURRY POWDER
1   CUP THINLY SLICED CELERY
¼   CUP FINELY CHOPPED GREEN ONION
1   SMALL PKG. TOASTED,
        SLIVERED ALMONDS
1   SMALL FRESH PINEAPPLE
     (OR ONE CAN DRAINED TIDBITS)
4   LARGE RIPE AVOCADOS
2   TBSPS. ITALIAN DRESSING

IN LARGE SAUCEPAN COMBINE CHICKEN, ONION, CELERY, SALT, PEPPER CORNS, BAY LEAF AND 4 CUPS OF WATER. BRING TO BOIL, REDUCE HEAT, SIMMER 30 MINUTES OR UNTIL CHICKEN IS TENDER. REMOVE FROM HEAT, LET CHICKEN COOL IN BROTH ONE HOUR. REMOVE SKIN AND DEBONE CHICKEN, THEN REFRIGERATE, COVERED, TWO HOURS OR OVERNIGHT. CONTINUED NEXT PAGE!

CURRIED CHICKEN BOATS

CONTINUED!

IN LARGE BOWL, COMBINE MAYONNAISE, HEAVY CREAM, CHUTNEY, CURRY AND ½ TSP. SALT. CUT CHICKEN IN CUBES, FOLD INTO DRESSING WITH SLICED CELERY, GREEN ONION AND ALMONDS. COVER, REFRIGERATE 2 HOURS OR OVERNIGHT.

BEFORE SERVING, PARE AND CORE PINEAPPLE. CUT INTO SMALL CUBES, AND FOLD INTO CHICKEN MIXTURE. (OR ADD CANNED PINEAPPLE TIDBITS). CUT AVOCADOS IN HALF LENGTHWISE, TWIST AND REMOVE PITS AND PEEL. BRUSH WITH ITALIAN DRESSING. FILL WITH CHICKEN SALAD AND PLACE ON LETTUCE LINED PLATES. SERVES 8.

THIS SOUNDS COMPLICATED, BUT IS WELL WORTH THE EFFORT. (SEE PICTURE.)

LIVE YOUR LIFE SO THAT YOU WON'T BE AFRAID TO BE THE FIRST WOMAN TO LEAVE A LADIES' BRIDGE PARTY.

TOMATO ASPIC

- 2 TSPS. CIDER OR RED WINE VINEGAR
- 1/2 TSP. EACH OF SALT, BASIL AND ACCENT
- 1 PKG. LEMON JELLO
- 1 CAN TOMATO SOUP AND WATER
  TO MAKE 2 CUPS LIQUID.
- 2 STALKS CELERY, CHOPPED
- 1 MEDIUM ONION (OR 3 GREEN ONIONS)
  CHOPPED FINE
- 4 CLOVES
- 1 HANDFUL FROZEN GREEN PEAS
- 1 CAN MEDIUM CLEANED SHRIMP

BRING JELLO AND LIQUID TO BOIL. ADD ALL INGREDIENTS EXCEPT SHRIMP AND CELERY AND COOK FOR 5 MINUTES. REMOVE CLOVES AND ADD SHRIMP AND CELERY.

POUR INTO LIGHTLY OILED MOLD AND CHILL UNTIL SET. SERVE ON LETTUCE LINED PLATE, GARNISHED WITH EXTRA SHRIMP, OLIVES AND MAYONNAISE, ALONG WITH CHEESE STICKS IF SERVING FOR BRIDGE.

OUT OF THE MOUTHS OF BABES TOO OFTEN, COMES CEREAL.

PICTURED ON PAGE 53;

CURRIED CHICKEN BOATS - 50

FLOWERS BY COLONIAL FLOWER SHOPPE, CALGARY

CHEESE STICKS

1½ to 2 cups "OLD" grated cheese
2   tsps. dry mustard
¼   tsp cayenne pepper
½   cup butter or margarine
1   cup flour
¼   cup water

Combine all ingredients. Mixture will be soft. Put into cookie press or roll out and cut in strips. Bake at 300° until lightly browned.

DENIAL IS A RIVER IN EGYPT.

FRUIT COCKTAIL SALAD

1   pkg. lemon jello
1   envelope dream whip, prepared
1   cup canned fruit cocktail,
        drained
1   cup miniature marshmallows
¼   cup mayonnaise

Prepare jello as directed. Let set until lightly jelled. Fold in remaining ingredients. Serve with hot cheese rolls.

CHICKEN GUMBO SALAD

- 2 CANS CHICKEN GUMBO SOUP
- 2 CANS SOLID TUNA OR
  2 TO 3 CUPS CUBED CHICKEN
- 1 CUP CHOPPED CELERY
- ½ CUP CHOPPED GREEN ONION
- 2 PKG. LEMON JELLO DISSOLVED IN
- 1 CUP BOILING WATER
- 1 CUP WHIPPING CREAM, WHIPPED
- 1 CUP MAYONNAISE

DISSOLVE JELLO IN BOILING WATER. ADD ALL INGREDIENTS EXCEPT CREAM AND MAYONNAISE. MIX WHIPPED CREAM AND MAYONNAISE AND ADD TO SALAD MIXTURE. POUR INTO INDIVIDUAL MOLDS AND REFRIGERATE UNTIL SET. SERVES 8.

MAN HAS GREAT NEED FOR WOMAN. NAPOLEON HAD HIS JOSEPHINE; ANTONY HAD HIS CLEOPATRA, AND EVEN HEINZ HAD HIS TOMATO.

Cottage Cheese Salad

1 PKG. LIME JELLO
1 CUP HOT WATER
1 TBSP. VINEGAR OR LEMON JUICE
1 TBSP. GRATED CARROT
1 TBSP. CHOPPED CELERY
1 TBSP. CHOPPED GREEN ONION
1 TBSP. CHOPPED GREEN OLIVES
½ CUP MAYONNAISE
½ CUP MILK
12 OZ. CARTON COTTAGE CHEESE

COMBINE JELLO, HOT WATER AND VINEGAR OR LEMON JUICE. REFRIGERATE UNTIL PARTIALLY SET. MEANWHILE, PREPARE CARROT, CELERY, GREEN ONIONS AND OLIVES. COMBINE MAYONNAISE AND MILK AND ADD VEGETABLES, AND COTTAGE CHEESE. FOLD MIXTURE INTO PARTIALLY SET JELLO AND POUR INTO LIGHTLY GREASED MOLD, REFRIGERATING UNTIL COMPLETELY SET.

THIS IS A GOOD SALAD BY ITSELF WITH HOT ROLLS, OR AS A COMPLEMENT TO TURKEY OR CHICKEN.

A MODERN GIRL IS ONE WHO DRESSES FIT TO KILL, AND COOKS THE SAME WAY.

BLENDER LEMONADE

2 TO 3 LEMONS
1 TO 2 CUPS WHITE SUGAR

CUT LEMONS INTO FOUR PIECES EACH AND PUT IN BLENDER CONTAINER, ADDING ABOUT 4 ICE CUBES. FILL BLENDER WITH COLD WATER, BLEND AND STRAIN.

YOU MAY VARY THE AMOUNT OF SUGAR ACCORDING TO YOUR OWN TASTE BUDS.

A MINOR OPERATION IS ONE PERFORMED ON SOMEBODY ELSE.

SPICED TEA

THIS MIXTURE CAN BE STORED IN A PLASTIC CONTAINER INDEFINITELY. GREAT WITH LATE SNACKS, ON THE SKI TRAIL, AT MEETINGS,- ANY TIME!

½ CUP INSTANT TEA
1½ CUPS SUGAR
2 PKGS. (3½ OZ. EACH) ORANGE TANG
1 TSP. CINNAMON
½ TSP. CLOVES

USE 2 TO 3 TSPS. PER CUP, ADD BOILING WATER.

EGGNOG SUPREME
(SEE PICTURE)

MAKE THIS A TRADITION ON CHRISTMAS
EVE OR SPLURGE AND ENTERTAIN THE
LADIES THE FRIDAY BEFORE. A WELCOME
RELIEF TO GET TOGETHER FOR AN AFTERNOON
CHAT AFTER SHOPPING. SAVE YOURSELF
FOR EGGNOG, SHERRY AND CHRISTMAS CAKE
AND GOODIES.

IN A LARGE PUNCH BOWL COMBINE:

    12 EGG YOLKS
     1 CUP GRANULATED SUGAR

BEAT TILL LEMON COLOURED AND THICK;
THEN SLOWLY ADD:

    13 OZ. BRANDY
    26 OZ. RYE OR RUM
     2 CUPS LIGHT CREAM

BEAT TO BLEND WELL AND CHILL ONE
HOUR OR OVERNIGHT TO ALLOW EGG TO MELLOW.

    12 EGG WHITES
     3 CUPS WHIPPING CREAM

BEAT EGG WHITES UNTIL STIFF. BEAT
3 CUPS CREAM IN LARGE BOWL, FOLD IN EGG
WHITES, THEN ADD TO EGG YOLK MIXTURE IN
PUNCH BOWL. SPRINKLE WITH GRATED
NUTMEG AND PLACE SPRIG OF HOLLY ON TOP.
PLACE CUPS AND LADLE BESIDE BOWL ON
COFFEE TABLE AND INVITE GUESTS TO HELP
THEMSELVES - THEY'LL ASK FOR SPOONS!

LEMONADE CONCENTRATE

A CONVENIENT SUMMER REFRESHER.

- 2 OZ. CITRIC ACID
- 1 OZ. TARTARIC ACID

BUY THEM AT A DRUG STORE.

- 5 LBS. WHITE SUGAR
- 6 CUPS WATER
- 6 LEMONS, WITH RIND OF 3

BRING WATER TO A BOIL, THROW IN ALL INGREDIENTS AND BOIL FOR 5 MINUTES. STRAIN INTO STERILIZED JARS. TO SERVE, ADD AMOUNT OF SYRUP DESIRED IN GLASS OR JUG WITH COLD WATER AND ICE CUBES, TO TASTE.

BRANDY MINT CREAM

THIS IS A TERRIFIC LIGHT DRINK TO SERVE INSTEAD OF DESSERT, EITHER AT BRIDGE OR AFTER A SPECIAL DINNER.

- 2 QUARTS FRENCH VANILLA ICE CREAM
- 4 OZ. CREME DE MENTHE
- 8 OZ. BRANDY

LET ICE CREAM SIT AT ROOM TEMPERATURE TO SOFTEN. BLEND ALL INGREDIENTS TOGETHER. SERVE IN STEM GLASS.
SEE PICTURE PAGE 17

II BUFFETS

18 LARGE WHOLE FRESH MUSHROOMS
2 TBSPS. VEGETABLE OIL
1 SMALL ONION, FINELY CHOPPED
1/4 LB. GROUND BEEF
2 SLICES HAM, COARSELY CHOPPED
1/3 CUP DRY SHERRY
1/4 CUP FINE BREAD CRUMBS
1 TSP. GARLIC POWDER
1 TSP. SALT
1/2 TSP. PEPPER
1/4 CUP GRATED PARMESAN CHEESE

CAREFULLY REMOVE STEMS FROM THE MUSHROOMS. CHOP STEMS FINELY AND RESERVE. PLACE MUSHROOM CAPS ON A COOKIE SHEET. HEAT OIL IN A LARGE SKILLET OVER MODERATE HEAT, COOK ONION AND BEEF UNTIL LIGHTLY BROWNED, STIRRING FREQUENTLY. ADD THE CHOPPED STEMS, HAM AND SHERRY TO ONION-BEEF MIXTURE AND COOK FIVE MINUTES. ADD BREAD CRUMBS, GARLIC POWDER, SALT AND PEPPER AND MIX WELL. STUFF MIXTURE INTO CAPS. SPRINKLE WITH CHEESE. BROIL MUSHROOMS IN PREHEATED BROILER, 3" FROM SOURCE OF HEAT 2 TO 5 MINUTES. SERVE HOT.

CRABMEAT DIP

1 CAN DRAINED CRABMEAT
½ CUP MAYONNAISE
2 TBSPS. CATSUP OR CHILI SAUCE
2 TO 3 TBSPS. LEMON JUICE
SEASONED PEPPER TO TASTE
GARLIC SALT OR POWDER TO TASTE
½ TSP. HORSERADISH

COMBINE ALL INGREDIENTS, MIXING WELL.
SERVE AS AN APPETIZER WITH COLD, FRESH
VEGETABLE TRAY, INCLUDING ZUCCHINI STICKS,
CAULIFLOWER CHUNKS, CARROT AND CELERY
STICKS, CHERRY TOMATOES.

AVOCADO DIP

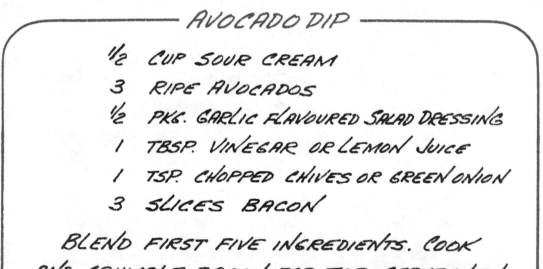

½ CUP SOUR CREAM
3 RIPE AVOCADOS
½ PKG. GARLIC FLAVOURED SALAD DRESSING
1 TBSP. VINEGAR OR LEMON JUICE
1 TSP. CHOPPED CHIVES OR GREEN ONION
3 SLICES BACON

BLEND FIRST FIVE INGREDIENTS. COOK
AND CRUMBLE BACON FOR TOP. SERVE WITH
VEGETABLE PLATTER OR CORN CHIPS.
THIS DOES NOT KEEP WELL AS THE
AVOCADO WILL DISCOLOUR.

THESE HAVE BEEN A PERENNIAL FAVOURITE, ESPECIALLY WITH THE MEN. BE SURE TO MAKE LOTS - A GUARANTEED SELL-OUT!

3	LBS. SMALL CHICKEN WINGS (ABOUT 15)
½	CUP SUGAR
3	TBSPS. CORNSTARCH
½	TSP. SALT
½	TSP. GROUND GINGER
¼	TSP. PEPPER
⅔	CUP WATER
⅓	CUP LEMON JUICE
¼	CUP SOYA SAUCE

CUT WINGS IN HALF AT JOINT. DISCARD TIPS. PLACE ON BROILER RACK AND BAKE AT 400° FOR 15 MINUTES, TURN AND BAKE ADDITIONAL 15 MINUTES. MIX THE SUGAR, CORNSTARCH, SALT, GINGER AND PEPPER. ADD LIQUIDS. COOK, STIRRING CONSTANTLY, OVER MEDIUM HEAT UNTIL MIXTURE THICKENS. BOIL 2 MINUTES. BRUSH OVER WINGS. CONTINUE BAKING AT 400° FOR ABOUT 35 MINUTES. DURING BAKING, BRUSH SOY MIXTURE ON WINGS FREQUENTLY. SERVE IN CHAFING DISH.

SEE PICTURE PAGE 71

Do all chopping first. This will take about 2 hours, but a blender shouldn't be used. Cook, stirring constantly, 10 minutes;

- 8 oz. Olive Oil
- 1 very large cauliflower, cut into bite size pieces
- 2 tins ripe olives, chopped
- 1 16 oz. tin broken green olives, chopped
- 2 12 oz. jars pickled onions, chopped

Add;

- 2 10 oz. tins mushroom stems and pieces
- 2 large green peppers, chopped
- 2 4 oz. tins pimento, chopped
- 4 15 oz. bottles Heinz catsup
- 1 15 oz. bottle Heinz 'Hot' catsup
- 1 48 oz. jar mixed pickles, chopped

Simmer 10 minutes and stir often. Drain and pour boiling water over the following to rinse;

- 2 tins anchovies, chopped
- 3 7 oz. tins solid tuna, chopped
- 3 tins small shrimp

Continued next page!

Antipasto

Continued!

Add anchovies, tuna and shrimp to mixture and place in sterilized jars and seal. PROCESS OR FREEZE. This is a great recipe to make with a friend and will cost about $35.00

Serve with crackers or chips. Really "superscrumbonious"

Beauty is only skin!

Blue Cheese Appetizers

Fast and easy for unexpected guests.

2 TBSPS. BUTTER
2 TBSPS. CRUMBLED BLUE CHEESE
1 PKG. REFRIGERATED BISCUITS

Preheat oven to 450°. Melt butter and add cheese stirring until smooth. Cut uncooked biscuits into quarters and place in pan touching together. Pour cheese mixture over top and bake approximately 10 minutes or until browned.

This may be frozen! Line 34 muffin cups with pastry. If you're in a hurry, use Robin Hood pie crust mix—it NEVER fails.

Filling:

- 6 slices crisp bacon, crumbled
- 2 oz. natural Swiss cheese
- 2 eggs
- 1 cup whipping cream
- ½ tsp. salt
- Pinch nutmeg
- 1 tsp. sugar
- Pinch pepper

Heat oven to 400°. Shred cheese. Combine eggs, cream, salt, nutmeg, sugar and pepper. Beat to blend well. Sprinkle bottom of each tart with bacon, then cheese. Fill each cup ¾ full with egg mixture. Sprinkle with nutmeg on top. Bake 10 minutes at 400° then 10 minutes longer at 350°.

Note: If frozen, reheat at 325°.

Weddings? For the bride a wedding means a shower; for the groom, it's curtains!

LIVER PÂTÉ

1 LB. CHICKEN LIVERS
1 ONION, SLICED
4 TBSPS GRATED ONION
1 TSP. DRY MUSTARD
2 TBSPS. DRY SHERRY
½ TO ¾ CUP SOFT BUTTER
PINCH OF MACE
SALT AND PEPPER

SIMMER CHICKEN LIVERS IN WATER WITH ONION, FOR ABOUT 20 MINUTES. DRAIN LIVERS AND REMOVE ONION. GRIND LIVERS VERY FINE. ADD REMAINING INGREDIENTS AND MIX WELL. SERVE AS AN HORS D'OUVRE WITH THINLY SLICED BROWN BREAD OR MELBA TOAST.

AS EVERY INTELLIGENT HUSBAND KNOWS, THE BEST TIME TO WASH THE DISHES IS RIGHT AFTER HIS WIFE TELLS HIM TO.

COUNTRY PÂTÉ

- 1 LB. GROUND VEAL
- 1/8 LB. PORK LIVER
- 1/2 LB. GROUND PORK
- 3 SLICES OF BACON
- 1/2 CUP CHOPPED ONION
- 1 TBSP. CHOPPED PARSLEY
- 1 1/2 TSP. SALT
- 1 TSP. PEPPER
- 1/3 TSP. GINGER
- 1/8 TSP. EACH, CLOVES AND CINNAMON
- 1 TSP. WORCESTERSHIRE SAUCE
- 2 DROPS TABASCO
- 1 TBSP. EACH, BRANDY AND MADEIRA
  (OR SHERRY)

COMBINE ALL INGREDIENTS EXCEPT BACON. BUTTER A LOAF PAN. PRESS MIXTURE AND TOP WITH BACON. COVER WITH OILED FOIL AND COOK AT 350° FOR 1 HOUR.

SERVE ONE OR TWO DAYS AFTER COOKING. MAY BE FROZEN. THIS IS GREAT WITH RYE BREAD, AS A BEFORE DINNER APPETIZER.

LOVE IS LIKE A MUSHROOM. YOU NEVER KNOW IF IT'S THE REAL THING UNTIL IT'S TOO LATE.

PICTURED ON PAGE 71;

DRUMSTICK CANAPES page 65

Hot Seafood Dip

1 8 oz. pkg. cream cheese
   at room temperature
1 6½ oz. tin crabmeat, tuna,
   or lobster
2 tbsps. chopped green onion
½ tsp. horseradish
⅓ cup slivered almonds
1 tbsp. milk
¼ tsp. salt
1 tbsp. lemon juice
chopped green pepper (optional)
dash of pepper

Combine all ingredients - except
almonds. Mix well. Garnish with almonds.
Warm in oven at 350° for 20 minutes.
Serve as a dip with crackers and chips.

When an eighty-four year old man
marries an eighty-year old woman,
don't throw rice. Throw vitamins.

A SPECIAL OCCASION APPETIZER TO SERVE WITH CRACKERS AND CHEESE TRAY, FOR EYE-APPEAL, SERVE IN CLEAR GLASS BOWL WITH TOOTHPICKS.

- 2 LBS. FROZEN JUMBO SHRIMP, PEELED AND DEVEINED
- ½ CUP CELERY LEAVES
- 3 TBSPS. MIXED PICKLING SPICES
- 1 TBSP. SALT
- 2 CUPS SLICED ONIONS
- SEVERAL BAY LEAVES
- 1 CUP SALAD OIL
- ¾ CUPS WHITE VINEGAR
- 3 TBSPS. CAPERS WITH JUICE
- 2½ TSPS. CELERY SEED
- 1½ TSPS. SALT
- 6 DROPS TABASCO SAUCE
- JUICE OF TWO LEMONS

IN LARGE POT COVER SHRIMP WITH BOILING WATER. ADD CELERY, PICKLING SPICES AND SALT. COVER AND SIMMER 5 MINUTES. DRAIN AND RINSE EACH SHRIMP UNDER COLD RUNNING WATER. LAYER SHRIMP, ONION AND BAY LEAVES IN SHALLOW DISH. COMBINE REMAINING INGREDIENTS. POUR OVER SHRIMP COVER AND CHILL AT LEAST 24 HOURS SPOONING THE MARINADE OVER OCCASIONALLY.

This is a delicious hot dip — a real hit for mid-winter get-togethers.

- 1 small onion - finely chopped
- 2 tbsps. butter
- 1 cup canned tomatoes, chopped and drained
- 1 can pickled green chilies, chopped
- 1 tsp. basil
- salt and freshly ground pepper, to taste
- 1/2 lb. Monterey Jack cheese - cubed
- 1 cup cream

Sauté onion in butter until transparent. Add tomatoes, chilies, basil, salt, and pepper. Simmer 15 minutes. Add cubed cheese and as it melts, stir in cream. Cook until blended and very smooth.

Serve hot from chafing dish or as a hot dip with strips of raw vegetables such as carrots, celery, green pepper, zucchini, or cauliflower chunks and artichoke hearts, as well as taco chips.

Is there life after birth?

ZIPPY AVOCADO DIP

- 1 LARGE AVOCADO
- 2 TBSPS. SLICED GREEN ONION
- 1 TBSP. LEMON JUICE
- 1 CUP MAYONNAISE
- 2 TBSPS. DAIRY SOUR CREAM
- 1 TSP. SUGAR
- 2 TSPS. WORCESTERSHIRE SAUCE
- 2 TSPS. SOY SAUCE
- 1/4 TSP. EACH, HOT PEPPER SAUCE, CELERY SEED AND DRY MUSTARD
- 1/8 TSP. WHITE PEPPER

PEEL AVOCADO AND DICE INTO BLENDER CONTAINER. ADD GREEN ONION AND LEMON JUICE AND BLEND UNTIL SMOOTH. ADD ALL REMAINING INGREDIENTS AND MIX WELL; CHILL. SERVE WITH POTATO OR CORN CHIPS. MAKES 2 TO 2 1/2 CUPS.

MOST KIDS ONLY EAT SPINACH SO THEY'LL GROW UP AND BE BIG AND STRONG ENOUGH TO TELL MOM WHAT SHE CAN DO WITH HER SPINACH.

OLIVE CHEESE PUFFS

- 24 STUFFED GREEN OLIVES (MAY ALSO USE GERKINS OR COCKTAIL ONIONS)
- ¼ CUP SOFT BUTTER
- 1 CUP SHARP CHEDDAR CHEESE, (GRATED)
- ¼ TSP. SALT
- ½ CUP FLOUR
- ½ TSP. PAPRIKA

BLEND CHEESE, BUTTER AND STIR IN FLOUR, SALT, PAPRIKA, MIXING WELL. MOLD DOUGH AROUND OLIVE. BAKE AT 400° FOR 10 MINUTES OR UNTIL GOLDEN. THESE MAY BE FROZEN AND REHEATED IN FOIL FOR 5 MINUTES AT 325°.

CHEESE STICKS

- 1½ TO 2 CUPS 'OLD' CHEDDAR CHEESE (GRATED)
- 2 TBSPS. DRY MUSTARD
- ¼ TSP. CAYENNE PEPPER
- ½ CUP BUTTER OR MARGARINE
- 1 CUP FLOUR
- ¼ CUP WATER

BLEND ABOVE INGREDIENTS INTO SOFT MIXTURE. PUT INTO COOKIE PRESS OR ROLL OUT AND CUT INTO STRIPS. BAKE AT 300° UNTIL LIGHTLY BROWNED.

CHICKEN BALLS
(A CHICKEN NEVER DOES!)

½ CUP FLOUR

1 TSP. ACCENT

1 TSP. SALT

1 OR 2 EGGS

2 TO 3 CHICKEN BREASTS OR
OTHER PIECES

CUT CHICKEN IN LONG, NARROW STRIPS AND ROLL INTO A BALL. ROLL CHICKEN PIECES IN EGG THEN DIP IN FLOUR FRY IN OIL UNTIL LIGHT BROWN.

SAUCE:

½ CUP SUGAR

½ CUP VINEGAR

1 TBSP. SOYA SAUCE

½ CUP PINEAPPLE CHUNKS

⅓ CUP PINEAPPLE JUICE

¼ CUP CATSUP

SPRINKLE PEPPER

2 TBSPS. CORNSTARCH

BOIL MIXTURE AND THICKEN WITH 2 TBSPS. CORNSTARCH. POUR OVER BALLS. BAKE 250° TO 275° FOR 1 HOUR. GREAT FOR A BUFFET!!

MISERY TO A WOMAN IS A LIVE SECRET AND A DEAD TELEPHONE.

POLYNESIAN CHICKEN

1 FRYER, CUT UP
¼ CUP SOYA SAUCE
3 TBSPS. VEGETABLE OIL
1 TSP. GINGER
2 TBSPS. MINCED ONION
½ CUP FLOUR
1 TIN PINEAPPLE CHUNKS
1 TIN MANDARIN ORANGES
2 TBSPS. CORNSTARCH
¼ CUP WATER
¼ CUP TOASTED SLIVERED ALMONDS

ARRANGE CHICKEN IN SHALLOW PAN. COMBINE SOYA SAUCE, OIL, GINGER, ONION AND MARINATE CHICKEN FOR ONE HOUR. SHAKE CHICKEN IN FLOUR AND BROWN IN OIL IN FRY PAN. DRAIN FRUIT AND SET ASIDE. ADD FRUIT JUICES TO SOYA MARINADE. PLACE CHICKEN IN CASSEROLE. POUR SOYA FRUIT SAUCE OVER AND BAKE IN A 350° OVEN FOR 45 MINUTES. SHORTLY BEFORE SERVING ADD FRUIT AND ALMONDS.

BEHIND EVERY GREAT MAN STANDS AN AMAZED MOTHER-IN-LAW.

SHRIMP STROGANOFF

- ¼ CUP MINCED ONION
- ¼ CUP BUTTER
- 1½ LBS. PEELED & DEVEINED SHRIMP
- ½ LB. MUSHROOMS (SLICED)
- 1 TBSP. FLOUR
- 1½ CUP SOUR CREAM
- 1¼ TSP. SALT
- PEPPER TO TASTE
- 1 TBSP. BUTTER

IN LARGE SKILLET SAUTÉ MINCED ONION IN ¼ CUP BUTTER UNTIL SOFTENED. ADD SHRIMP - SAUTÉ FOR 3 TO 5 MINUTES OR UNTIL PINK AND JUST COOKED. TRANSFER MIXTURE TO HEATED DISH AND KEEP WARM. ADD TO SKILLET MUSHROOMS AND 1 TBSP. BUTTER. SAUTÉ OVER MEDIUM HIGH HEAT UNTIL BROWNED. SPRINKLE FLOUR AND COOK, STIRRING FOR TWO (2) MINUTES. REDUCE HEAT TO MEDIUM-LOW AND STIR IN SHRIMP MIXTURE, SOUR CREAM (AT ROOM TEMPERATURE). ADD SALT AND PEPPER. COOK, STIRRING FOR 2 TO 3 MINUTES OR UNTIL SHRIMP ARE HEATED THROUGH. DO NOT BOIL! (SEE PICTURE)

GIRLS - KEEP CALM, COOL AND COLLECT!

CHICKEN CASSEROLE

- 2 CUPS CHICKEN, COOKED AND CUBED
- 1 CUP CHOPPED CELERY
- 1 CUP CHOPPED NUTS,
    (TOASTED, SLIVERED ALMONDS)
- 2 CUPS COOKED RICE
- 1 CUP MAYONNAISE
- 2 TBSPS. CHOPPED ONIONS
- 1 CAN CREAM OF CHICKEN SOUP
- 1 CAN CREAM OF MUSHROOM SOUP
- 3/4 TSP. SALT
- 3/4 TSP. PEPPER
- 2 TBSPS. LEMON JUICE
- 2 CHICKEN BOUILLON CUBES
    DISSOLVED IN 1/2 CUP WATER

COMBINE ALL INGREDIENTS, MIXING THOROUGHLY. PLACE IN A CASSEROLE. COVER WITH CRUSHED POTATO CHIPS AND ALMONDS. BAKE AT 400° FOR 45 MINUTES, OR UNTIL HEATED THROUGH. SERVES EIGHT.

THE HONEYMOON IS REALLY OVER WHEN HE PHONES TO SAY HE'LL BE LATE FOR DINNER, AND SHE HAS ALREADY LEFT A NOTE TO SAY IT'S IN THE REFRIGERATOR.

I HAVE A FRIEND WHO WOULD COME OVER ANY TIME OF THE DAY OR NIGHT FOR THIS MALAYSIAN DISH. (SECRETLY, I THINK HE LIKES THE CONDIMENTS BEST!) IT'S A BIT OF A PRODUCTION BUT THE ACCOLADES MAKE UP FOR THE EFFORT.   SERVES EIGHT.

4	TBSPS. BUTTER
2	CUPS CHOPPED (FINE) ONIONS
1	MINCED GARLIC CLOVE
2	TSP. SALT
2	TSP. POWDERED GINGER
1	TSP. GROUND CORIANDER
2	TBSP. GROUND ALMONDS
1/4	TSP. CUMIN SEED
3/4	TSP. DRIED GROUND CHILI PEPPERS
1	TSP. TUMERIC
1	19 OZ. CAN TOMATOES
1	TBSP. CORNSTARCH
2	CUPS COCONUT MILK (POUR BOILING WATER OVER 1 PKG. UNSWEETENED, SHREDDED COCONUT AND LET STAND 1 HOUR. STRAIN COCONUT; RESERVE LIQUID)
1	LB. LOBSTER, SHRIMP OR CRAB, CUBED
2	CUCUMBERS PEELED AND CUBED
1	TBSP. LIME OR LEMON JUICE
1	TSP. SUGAR

CONTINUED NEXT PAGE!

CONTINUED!

PREPARE COCONUT MILK. MELT BUTTER IN A SAUCEPAN. SAUTÉ ONIONS AND GARLIC UNTIL CLEAR. STIR IN SALT, GINGER, CORIANDER, ALMONDS, CUMIN, CHILI PEPPERS, TUMERIC AND TOMATOES. COVER AND COOK OVER LOW HEAT 4 MINUTES. SPRINKLE WITH CORNSTARCH AND GRADUALLY ADD COCONUT MILK, STIRRING CONSTANTLY UNTIL THICKENED. ADD SEAFOOD AND COOK OVER LOW HEAT 10 MINUTES, ADD CUCUMBERS, LIME JUICE AND SUGAR. COOK 5 MINUTES. SERVE OVER RICE. (BROWN RICE IS BEST.)

CONDIMENTS TO SERVE WITH CURRY;

1. BANANAS IN GINGER SAUCE

SQUEEZE JUICE OF ONE LEMON. ADD SUGAR AND GINGER TO TASTE. POUR OVER 2 OR 3 BANANAS SLICED INTO STRIPS.

2. MANDARIN ORANGES IN COCONUT

DRAIN ONE CAN MANDARIN ORANGES. ROAST COCONUT (1/3 CUP) AND SUGAR (2 TSP.) UNDER BROILER. POUR HOT COCONUT OVER MANDARIN ORANGES AND MIX.

IF YOU CAN SLEEP LIKE A BABY, YOU DON'T HAVE ONE.

This is a special dish and requires special care. It __must__ be cooked slowly at low heat or it will separate. It also suffers with reheating - so serve immediately. Serves six.

- ⅓ cup butter
- 2 tbsps. flour
- 2 cups cream
- 4 slightly beaten egg yolks
- 2 5oz. cans lobster
- 1 cup sliced, fresh mushrooms (sautéed)
- ¼ cup sherry
- 2 tsp. lemon juice
- ¼ tsp. salt
- 6 pattie shells (frozen or fresh)

In double boiler, melt butter and blend in flour. Gradually stir in cream. Cook slowly, stirring constantly until thickened. Stir small amount of sauce into egg yolks. Return to hot mixture and cook, stirring constantly for one minute. Add lobster, sherry, lemon juice and salt and mushrooms. Heat through and stir. Do not boil! Serve over pattie shells. Sprinkle with paprika and garnish with celery and black olives.

SCALLOPS IN WINE

ALWAYS A HIT - AND YOU CAN MAKE IT AHEAD.
SERVES EIGHT:

- 2 LBS. SCALLOPS
- 2 CUPS DRY WHITE WINE
- ¼ CUP BUTTER
- 4 FINELY CHOPPED SHALLOTS
- 24 FINELY SLICED MUSHROOM CAPS
- 2 TBSPS. MINCED PARSLEY
- 2 TBSPS FLOUR
- 2 TO 4 TBSPS. HEAVY CREAM
- BREAD CRUMBS

WASH SCALLOPS WELL. SIMMER IN WINE ABOUT 5 MINUTES. DRAIN AND RESERVE THE LIQUID. MELT BUTTER AND SAUTÉ SHALLOTS, MUSHROOM CAPS, PARSLEY. STIR IN FLOUR UNTIL BLENDED. ADD RESERVED LIQUID AND HEAVY CREAM. ADD SCALLOPS TO HOT SAUCE. PLACE IN SHALLOW CASSEROLE OR INDIVIDUAL SCALLOP SHELLS AND COVER WITH DRY BREAD CRUMBS. DOT WITH BUTTER AND PLACE UNDER BROILER UNTIL GOLDEN BROWN.

GIVE A BOY ENOUGH ROPE AND HE'LL BRING HOME A STRAY DOG ON THE END OF IT.

SERVES EIGHT. A TASTY DISH TO SERVE TO THE LADIES FOR LUNCH OR BRIDGE THAT CAN BE REHEATED.

- 8 PATTIE SHELLS (PEPPERIDGE FARM FROZEN PATTIE SHELLS ARE SUPER - RIGHT THERE IN YOUR FREEZER - AND THEY NEVER FAIL!)
- 1 LB. SMALL COOKED SHRIMP OR KING CRAB OR LOBSTER
- 1½ CUP SLICED FRESH MUSHROOMS
- 1 TBSP. CHOPPED FRESH PARSLEY
- ½ CUP SHERRY
- 4 TBSPS. BUTTER
- 4 TBSPS. FLOUR
- 2 CUPS MILK.

SALT AND PEPPER TO TASTE

BROWN MUSHROOMS IN 2 TBSPS. BUTTER. PREPARE WHITE SAUCE: MELT BUTTER OVER LOW HEAT. ADD AND BLEND FLOUR - COOK AT LEAST 3 MINUTES. STIR IN MILK SLOWLY. CONTINUE STIRRING TILL SAUCE IS SMOOTH AND THICKENED. ADD SHERRY. ADD SEAFOOD, COOKED MUSHROOMS AND PARSLEY. HEAT THROUGH. SERVE OVER PATTIES AND GARNISH WITH A SPRIG OF PARSLEY, RIPE OLIVES, CARROT CURLS AND CELERY STICKS. TO REHEAT - PLACE OVER DOUBLE BOILER.

CHINESE PORK ROAST

1 TBSP. SUGAR
1 TBSP. HONEY
3 TBSPS. CHICKEN BOUILLON
1 TSP. SALT
1 TBSP. SOY SAUCE
2 LBS. FRESH PORK BUTT OR SHOULDER OF PORK, CUT IN 3 PIECES, LENGTHWISE.

MIX THE MARINADE TOGETHER IN BOWL UNTIL WELL COMBINED. SOAK PORK FOR 3/4 OF AN HOUR, IN MARINADE, TURNING OCCASIONALLY. REMOVE FROM BOWL AND PLACE ON RACK IN A ROASTING PAN, ADDING A FEW TABLESPOONS OF WATER TO PREVENT FROM SMOKING. ROAST IN MODERATE OVEN AT 350° FOR ABOUT 1½ HOURS, TURNING OCCASIONALLY. SLICE PORK AND SERVE IMMEDIATELY WITH HOT MUSTARD.

YOU DON'T HAVE TO EAT AN APPLE A DAY TO KEEP THE DOCTOR AWAY. HE WON'T COME TO THE HOUSE, ANYHOW.

TOURTIÈRES

This is a very old French Canadian recipe for meat pies. It is particularly good because the meat is chopped, not ground, and most of the fat has been removed. This recipe usually makes about six pies, but this can vary with the amount of meat used. Always use a combination pork (or ham) and beef. The addition of breast of chicken lends a fuller flavor. Several pies can be prepared and frozen uncooked in DEEP aluminum pie pans (9" x 1½".) Always serve with rhubarb relish, recipe included. A tourtière and a jar of relish is a special gift at Christmas time. This takes lots of time, so proceed at a leisurely pace and enjoy yourself (a glass of wine helps.)

6 LBS. OF MEAT (THIS SHOULD BE A TOTAL WEIGHT AFTER REMOVAL OF BONE & FAT. START WITH APPROX. 12 LBS.)
PORK (BOSTON BUTT) OR FRESH HAM, — OR MIXTURE OF BOTH
BEEF - POT ROAST
CHICKEN - BREAST OF SMALL CHICKEN
BUTTER - ENOUGH TO BROWN ALL MEAT
1 TBSP. ALLSPICE
1 TBSP. SAVORY

RECIPE CONTINUED NEXT PAGE!

PICTURED ON PAGE 89;

ORIENTAL MEATBALLS PAGE 94
SHRIMP STROGANOFF PAGE 80

FLOWERS BY COLONIAL FLOWER SHOPPE, CALGARY.

CONTINUED!

2 MEDIUM SIZED ONIONS
1 CUP BREAD OR CRACKER CRUMBS
SALT, PEPPER, CHILI POWDER,
POULTRY SEASONING TO TASTE

CUT MEAT INTO BITE SIZED CUBES, REMOVING ALL EXCESS FAT. BROWN MEAT IN BUTTER, ADD SEASONING. COVER WITH HOT WATER AND SIMMER UNCOVERED FOR 3 HOURS. ALLOW TO COOL. SKIM OFF ANY EXCESS FAT. DRAIN OFF WATER, CORRECT SEASONING, AND PLACE IN UNBAKED PIE SHELLS. BAKE AT 350° UNTIL CRUST IS GOLDEN.

NOTE: FOR RHUBARB RELISH TO SERVE WITH THIS RECIPE, SEE NEXT PAGE!

ONE OF THE MAJOR PROBLEMS FACING THIS COUNTRY TODAY IS THAT TOO MANY WOMEN GET ALL EXCITED ABOUT NOTHING. ....AND THEN MARRY HIM.

RHUBARB RELISH

This makes approximately four half pints, and it's very easy

- 2 qts. cut rhubarb (8 cups)
- 1 cup chopped cooking onions
- 1/2 tsp. cinnamon
- 1/2 tsp. allspice
- 1/2 tsp. cloves
- 1 cup vinegar (white)
- 2 cups white sugar
- 1 tbsp. salt

Simmer uncovered approximately 4 hours (sometimes more) until quite thick. Watch closely as it burns easily. Pour into hot, sterile half pint jars and seal immediately (wax is not necessary on top).

Middle-age is when the phone rings on a Saturday night and you hope that it's the wrong number.

WILD RICE BROCCOLI CASSEROLE

This dish complements any meat or fowl, and don't turn your nose up at the tinned soup and rice mix - I know lots of really elegant ladies who prefer it to their caterer's fare!

- ½ lb. cheddar cheese, grated
- 2 heads broccoli (approx. 2 lbs.)
- 1 pkg. Uncle Ben's wild rice mixture
- 2 tins (or less) mushroom soup

Cook rice mixture as directed. Cook broccoli until crunchy. Mix soup and cheese. Butter the casserole dish. Alternate cheese-soup mixture, broccoli and rice in layers. Sprinkle with additional grated cheese. Cook at 350° for one hour.

A baby first laughs at the age of four weeks. By that time his eyes focus well enough to see you clearly.

½ CUP COOKING OIL

1½ LBS. GROUND BEEF

1 SMALL CLOVE GARLIC, CRUSHED

1 TSP. SALT

¼ TSP. PEPPER

2 EGGS

¼ CUP FLOUR

1 TSP. SALT

¼ TSP. PEPPER

½ CUP CHICKEN STOCK (OR BOUILLON)

1 14 OZ. CAN PINEAPPLE CHUNKS,
    DRAINED, RESERVE JUICE

3 TBSPS. CORNSTARCH

½ CUP SUGAR

½ CUP PINEAPPLE JUICE

½ CUP VINEGAR

3 TBSPS. SOY SAUCE

OPTIONAL:

1 LARGE TOMATO, PEELED AND CHOPPED

2 LARGE GREEN PEPPERS, 1" SQUARES

HEAT OIL IN FRYING PAN. COMBINE BEEF, GARLIC, SALT AND PEPPER; SHAPE INTO SIZE OF MEATBALLS DESIRED. BEAT EGGS, FLOUR, SALT AND PEPPER TOGETHER, ADDING WATER IF NECESSARY TO MAKE THIN BATTER.

CONTINUED NEXT PAGE!

Continued!

Dip meat balls in batter with tongs, shaking off excess and drop into hot oil. Cook slowly to brown on all sides. Remove meatballs as they brown and discard all but 1 tbsp. of oil as well as any pieces of batter. Add chicken stock, green pepper, if desired, and pineapple chunks to pan. Cover and simmer 5 minutes. Return meat to pan and simmer 3 minutes more. Mix cornstarch, sugar, pineapple juice, vinegar and soy sauce together until smooth. Add to pan, stirring constantly, until thickened. If serving tomato pieces, add just before serving.

These may be made as appetizers and kept warm in a chafing dish, or served as an entree over rice. This will freeze well and may be made well in advance. Serves 6 to 8.

(See picture page 89)

You cannot make a husband tender by keeping him in hot water.

A DELICIOUS VARIATION OF CHILI!

- 1 LB. GROUND BEEF
- 6 SLICES BACON
- 1 ONION, CHOPPED
- 1 GREEN PEPPER
- 1 CLOVE GARLIC
- 2 TBSPS. MOLASSES
- 2 TBSPS. BROWN SUGAR
- 1 TSP. DRY MUSTARD
- 1/3 CUP VINEGAR
- 1 19 OZ. CAN TOMATOES
- 1 CAN KIDNEY BEANS
- 1 CAN LIMA BEANS, DRAINED
- 1 CAN PORK AND BEANS
- 1 TSP. WORCESTERSHIRE SAUCE

SALT, PEPPER AND TABASCO SAUCE, TO TASTE.

FRY BACON TILL CRISP AND CRUMBLE. BROWN GROUND BEEF AND ONION. COMBINE BACON, GROUND BEEF AND ONION AND REMAINING INGREDIENTS IN A LARGE CASSEROLE. BAKE 2 TO 2½ HOURS AT 300°

A HUSBAND WHO GETS HIS BREAKFAST IN BED IS IN THE HOSPITAL.

Chinese Steak

Prepare your ingredients and cook this at the table in a wok with your guests looking on. Use round or sirloin steak. You can use electric fry pan or wok.

- 1 LB. STEAK (STRIPS 1/4" THICK)
- 1/2 TSP. GINGER, SALT AND PEPPER
- 1/4 CUP SALAD OIL
- 1 GREEN PEPPER, COARSELY CHOPPED
- 1 CUP CELERY, COARSELY CHOPPED
- 1/2 CUP ONION, COARSELY CHOPPED

SAUCE:

- 2 TBSPS. CORNSTARCH
- 1/3 CUP SOYA SAUCE
- 1 CUP HOT WATER
- 1 CUBE BEEF BOUILLON

Brown meat in fry pan and push to one side. Add vegetables and stir fry. Pour sauce over and simmer. Lastly, add chunks of tomatoes and serve on rice.

Marriage is a lot like a boxing event.... Sometimes the preliminaries are better than the main event.

CHICKEN FRIED RICE

2   TBSPS. COOKING OIL
3   CUPS COOKED RICE
1   MEDIUM ONION, CHOPPED FINE
1   EGG
½ TO 1 CUP DICED MEAT, RAW OR COOKED
2   CHOPPED GREEN ONIONS
SALT
SOY SAUCE TO TASTE

IN A LARGE, HEAVY SKILLET, HEAT AT HIGH TEMPERATURE 2 TBSPS. OF COOKING OIL. WHEN HOT, ADD MEAT AND ONION. FRY UNTIL COOKED. BREAK EGG INTO MEAT MIXTURE AND SCRAMBLE, STIRRING CONSTANTLY. TURN HEAT TO LOW, ADD RICE, SALT AND SOY SAUCE TO SUIT YOUR TASTE. BEFORE SERVING ADD GREEN ONIONS. THIS SHOULD BE SERVED IMMEDIATELY, BUT MAY BE KEPT WARM IN CHAFING DISH. SERVES 6.

THE DOCTORS ARE SAYING THAT DRINKING IS BAD FOR US. I DON'T KNOW. YOU SEE A LOT MORE OLD DRUNKS THAN OLD DOCTORS.

Sweet 'N Sour Ribs

2 lbs. ribs, browned

Sauce:

3/4 cup brown sugar

1/2 cup catsup

1/2 cup vinegar

3/4 cup water

2 tbsps. Worcestershire Sauce

1/2 tsp. chili powder

1 onion, diced

salt, pepper

Pour over ribs and bake in a 250° oven for three (3) hours, uncovered.

Childhood is that wonderful time when all you have to do to lose weight is to take a bath.

Dry Ribs

Dip desired amount of ribs, which have been cut into 1" pieces, into soy sauce and then into flour and salt and pepper. Fry in deep fat at 385° until done.

2½ INCH SIRLOIN STEAK

SALT AND FRESHLY GROUND PEPPER,
   (TO TASTE)

1 MEDIUM ONION, FINELY CHOPPED

1 CUP CATSUP

3 TBSPS. BUTTER, MELTED

1 TBSP. LEMON JUICE

1 SMALL GREEN PEPPER, SLICED

FRESH CHOPPED PARSLEY,
   (1 SMALL BUNCH)

FEW DROPS WORCESTERSHIRE SAUCE

PREHEAT BROILER. PLACE STEAK 4" BELOW BROILER. SEAR BOTH SIDES. REMOVE AND DRAIN FAT. SEASON WITH SALT AND PEPPER. MIX ALL INGREDIENTS AND POUR OVER STEAK IN PAN. PLACE IN 425° OVEN FOR 30 MINUTES. REMOVE FROM OVEN. POUR MUSTARD SAUCE OVER AND SPRINKLE PARSLEY ON TOP AND SERVE.

FOR MUSTARD SAUCE, SEE NEXT PAGE!

THE MAN WHO SAYS THAT MARRIAGE IS A 50-50 PROPOSITION DOESN'T UNDERSTAND TWO THINGS 1.) WOMEN, 2) FRACTIONS.

MUSTARD SAUCE

(FOR BAKED STEAK)

- 2 TBSPS. BUTTER
- 2 TBSPS. BAR-B-QUE SAUCE, (ANY COMMERCIAL BRAND)
- 2 TSPS. WORCESTERSHIRE SAUCE
- 2 TSPS. DRY MUSTARD
- 2 TBSPS. CREAM.

MIX ALL INGREDIENTS EXCEPT CREAM TO MELTED BUTTER. HEAT OVER MEDIUM HEAT. ADD CREAM AND HEAT AGAIN OVER MEDIUM HEAT.

FRANKS IN SILVER

- 2 CUPS MINCED FRANKFURTERS
- 1/4 CUP GRATED CHEESE
- 1 1/2 TSPS. PREPARED MUSTARD
- 2 HARD BOILED EGGS, CHOPPED
- 1 TSP. WORCESTERSHIRE SAUCE
- 2 TBSPS. SWEET PICKLE RELISH
- 1/4 TSP. CHILI POWDER
- 2 TBSPS. MAYONNAISE

COMBINE MINCED FRANKFURTERS AND NEXT INGREDIENTS. FILL FRANKFURTER ROLLS. WRAP SECURELY IN FOIL. PLACE ON BARBECUE FOR 15 TO 20 MINUTES. TURN OFTEN.

STUFFED CHICKEN BREASTS
WITH MUSHROOM SAUCE

4 TO 6 DE-BONED CHICKEN BREASTS

2 CUPS BREAD CRUMBS

2 TBSPS. MELTED BUTTER

2 TBSPS ONION

1 TSP. SALT

1/4 TSP. POULTRY SEASONING

1/4 CUP HOT WATER

HALVE BREASTS AND DUST WITH FLOUR, SALT AND PAPRIKA. COMBINE OTHER INGREDIENTS, STUFF BREASTS AND HOLD WITH TOOTHPICK IF NECESSARY. BROWN IN BUTTER IN FRY PAN. BAKE IN OVEN AT 325° FOR 1 HOUR.

SERVE WITH MUSHROOM SAUCE.

MUSHROOM SAUCE:

1/2 LB. FRESH MUSHROOMS

2 TBSPS. BUTTER

1/4 CUP MINCED ONION

2 TBSPS. FLOUR

1/2 CUP SOUR CREAM

1/2 PINT WHIPPING CREAM

SALT AND PEPPER

BROWN MUSHROOMS AND ONION. STIR IN FLOUR, SALT AND PEPPER. COOK VERY SLOWLY ADDING CREAM AND SOUR CREAM. POUR OVER CHICKEN JUST BEFORE SERVING.

SATURDAY NIGHT SPECIAL

½ LB. SPAGHETTI

1 LB. MINCED BEEF

1 14 OZ. CAN NIBLETS CORN

1 CUP GRATED CHEESE

1 CAN TOMATO SOUP

1 14 OZ. CAN TOMATOES

1 SMALL ONION, MINCED

1 GREEN PEPPER, MINCED

¾ TSP. SALT

½ TSP. CHILI POWDER

½ TSP. WORCESTERSHIRE SAUCE

½ LB. MUSHROOMS

IN FRYING PAN BROWN GREEN PEPPER, MUSHROOMS AND MEAT. BREAK SPAGHETTI INTO PIECES AND BOIL IN SALTED WATER UNTIL TENDER. (15 MINUTES) COMBINE ALL INGREDIENTS IN LARGE BOWL. MIX WELL. BAKE IN MODERATE OVEN (325°) FOR 45 MINUTES. SERVES 6 TO 8

TOMORROW IS TODAY'S GREATEST LABOUR - SAVING DEVICE.

LASAGNE

EVERYONE HAS A LASAGNE RECIPE, BUT
THIS IS OUR FAVORITE:

- 1½ LB. GROUND BEEF
- 1 28 OZ. CAN TOMATOES
- 1 14 OZ. CAN SEASONED TOMATO SAUCE
- 2 ENVELOPES SPAGHETTI SAUCE MIX
- 2 CLOVES GARLIC, MINCED
- 8 OZ. LASAGNE OR BROAD NOODLES
- 2 6 OR 8 OZ. PKG. THIN SLICED
    MOZZARELLA CHEESE
- 1 CUP CREAMED COTTAGE CHEESE
- ½ CUP GRATED PARMESAN CHEESE

BROWN MEAT SLOWLY; DRAIN OFF EXCESS
FAT. ADD NEXT FOUR INGREDIENTS. COVER
AND SIMMER 40 MINUTES, STIRRING
OCCASIONALLY. SALT TO TASTE. COOK NOODLES
IN BOILING SALTED WATER UNTIL TENDER
FOLLOWING PACKAGE INSTRUCTIONS. DRAIN.
RINSE IN COLD WATER. PLACE ½ NOODLES
IN 9"x13" BAKING DISH. COVER WITH ⅓
SAUCE, THEN LAYER ½ MOZZARELLA AND
½ COTTAGE CHEESE. REPEAT LAYERS
ENDING WITH SAUCE. TOP WITH PARMESAN
BAKE AT 350° FOR 25 TO 30 MINUTES.
LET STAND 15 MINUTES. CUT IN SQUARES.
SERVE WITH GREEN SALAD & FRENCH BREAD.
SERVES 6 TO 8.

Rice Casserole

3 to 4 slices bacon
1/2 cup minced onion
1 cup diced celery
1/2 green pepper, chopped (optional)
1 can mushroom soup
1/2 can water
2 cups rice
1 tsp. salt

Cook rice. Cook the bacon until crisp, break into crumbs. Cook the onion, celery and green pepper in the bacon fat until the celery is tender. Drain. Mix all the ingredients in a casserole dish. Bake at 300° for 1 hour. This will serve six.

If you have trouble going to sleep at night, lie at the very edge of the bed.....you'll soon drop off.

JAPANESE CHICKEN WINGS

3	LBS. CHICKEN WINGS
1	BEATEN EGG
1	CUP FLOUR
1	CUP BUTTER

CUT WINGS IN HALF. DIP IN SLIGHTLY BEATEN EGG AND THEN IN FLOUR. FRY IN BUTTER UNTIL DEEP BROWN AND CRISP. PUT IN SHALLOW ROASTING PAN AND POUR SAUCE OVER WINGS.

SAUCE:

3	TBSPS. SOYA SAUCE
3	TBSPS. WATER
1	CUP WHITE SUGAR
½	CUP VINEGAR
1	TSP. ACCENT
½	TSP. SALT

BAKE AT 350° FOR ½ HOUR. SPOON SAUCE OVER WINGS DURING COOKING.

GREAT FOR CROWDS, KIDS AND SNACKS. TASTES GOOD WARMED UP IF THERE ARE ANY LEFT OVER.

WHO EVER SAID, "WHERE THERE'S SMOKE, THERE'S FIRE," MUST NEVER HAVE OWNED A FIREPLACE.

VERY QUICK — AND VERY GOOD!

- 2 PKGS. CUT UP CHICKEN
- 6 TBSPS. OIL
- 2 CUPS SLICED FRESH MUSHROOMS
- 1 CAN MUSHROOM SOUP
- ½ CUP CHICKEN BROTH
- ½ CUP ORANGE JUICE
- ½ CUP DRY WHITE WINE (OR VERMOUTH)
- 1 TBSP. BROWN SUGAR
- ½ TSP. SALT
- 4 CARROTS, SLICED JULIENNE STYLE

SHAKE CHICKEN IN SEASONED FLOUR AND FRY IN OIL. FRY MUSHROOMS IN BUTTER. COMBINE REMAINING INGREDIENTS IN LARGE CASSEROLE. ADD CHICKEN AND MUSHROOMS. COOK AT 350° FOR 1 HOUR.

SERVE OVER RICE WITH A FRESH GREEN SALAD.

IN PREPARING A DISH FOR BEDTIME, CHAMPAGNE MAKES THE BEST TENDERIZER.

TURKEY CASSEROLE WITH BROCCOLI

- 2 CUPS NOODLES
- 1 PKG. FROZEN BROCCOLI
- 2 CUPS COOKED TURKEY
- 1/3 CUP SLIVERED ALMONDS

FOR WHITE SAUCE:

- 2 TBSPS. BUTTER
- 2 TBSPS. FLOUR
- 1 TSP. SALT
- 1/4 TSP. PREPARED MUSTARD
- 1/4 TSP. PEPPER
- 2 CUPS MILK
- 1 CUP GRATED CHEDDAR CHEESE

HEAT OVEN TO 350°. COOK NOODLES, THEN BROCCOLI. MAKE WHITE SAUCE; WHEN THICK STIR IN CHEESE. DICE BROCCOLI STEMS LEAVING FLOWERS FOR TOP. PUT NOODLES, BROCCOLI STEMS, TURKEY AND ALMONDS IN CASSEROLE. COVER WITH SAUCE. ARRANGE BROCCOLI FLOWERS ON TOP AND BAKE FOR 15 TO 20 MINUTES.

A FEEDSTORE IS ABOUT THE ONLY PLACE THESE DAYS WHERE YOU CAN GET A CHICKEN DINNER FOR A DIME.

Very mild – even the children like this one.

- 2 frozen pkg. chicken wings
- seasoned flour
- 6 tbsps. cooking oil
- 1 medium onion, chopped
- 1 tsp. curry powder
- 2 chicken bouillon cubes
- 3 tbsps. flour
- 1½ cups water

Remove tips of chicken wings. Shake in seasoned flour and brown in cooking oil. Remove chicken to casserole and sprinkle with chopped onion. Make gravy in frying pan using water, flour, chicken bouillon cubes and curry. Pour over chicken and bake at 325° for 1½ hours

Good vegetable accompaniment: carrots and celery, sliced julienne style, cooked together in small amount of water, served in butter.

Mealtime? When the kids sit down to continue eating.

Great with a green salad after a late night bridge.

- 2 cans crab (6½ oz.)
- 1 tbsp. lemon juice
- 4 tbsrs. butter
- 4 tbsps. flour
- 2 cups milk
- 1 tsp. salt
- ½ tsp. pepper
- 1 tsp. curry powder
- ¾ cup grated cheddar
- 1½ cups. cooked flat noodles, drained
- ½ cup crumbled potato chips

Flake crab; sprinkle with lemon juice. Melt butter over low heat. Add and blend flour. Cook at least 3 minutes. Stir in milk slowly. Continue stirring until sauce is smooth, thickened. Add seasonings. Add ½ cup cheese to sauce. Add crab and noodles and spoon into buttered 2 quart casserole. Top with crumbled chips and remaining cheese. Bake at 350° for 30 minutes. Serves 6.

Two can live as cheaply as one large family used to.

This recipe may be used as an appetizer or evening bridge menu, doubled, served along with hot rolls and a beverage.

- ¼ cup butter or margarine, (melted)
- ½ cup grated parmesan cheese
- ½ cup dry bread crumbs
- ¼ cup lemon juice
- ⅔ cup chopped green onions
- 1 garlic clove, minced
- ¼ tsp. salt
- 1 lb. cooked, peeled, deveined shrimp
- Fresh parsley

Combine all ingredients. Place in four individual shells or casseroles. Bake at 350° for 20 to 25 minutes. Garnish with parsley.

Don't try to make ends meet. Just about the time you manage to make ends meet.... your wife moves the ends.

SHRIMP IN FOIL

2 PKG. CHOPPED (FROZEN) SPINACH
1½ LBS. SHRIMP (FROZEN COOKED)
¼ CUP BUTTER OR MARGARINE
¼ CUP FLOUR
1½ CUPS MILK
½ CUP WHITE WINE
½ CUP SCALLIONS (OR GREEN ONION)
SALT, PEPPER, PAPRIKA
1 CUP SHREDDED CHEDDAR CHEESE

PREHEAT OVEN 350°. LINE 9" PIE PAN WITH HEAVY FOIL. THAW AND DRAIN SPINACH. SPREAD IN PAN AND TOP WITH SHRIMP. IN SAUCE PAN, MELT BUTTER AND STIR IN FLOUR. ADD MILK GRADUALLY WITH WINE AND ONIONS. COOK, STIRRING CONSTANTLY OVER LOW HEAT UNTIL SAUCE BUBBLES AND THICKENS. ADD SALT, PEPPER TO TASTE AND ENOUGH PAPRIKA TO MAKE A ROSY COLOUR. POUR OVER SHRIMP AND SPRINKLE WITH CHEESE. BAKE IN OVEN 35 MINUTES OR UNTIL BUBBLY.

THIS MAY BE MADE AHEAD AND FROZEN. WHEN READY TO USE, BAKE UNCOVERED FOR 1 HOUR.

CHINESE HAMBURGER

CASUAL, DELICIOUS AND VERY EASY TO MAKE.
SERVES SIX.

- 1 CAN CREAM OF MUSHROOM SOUP
- 1 CAN CREAM OF CHICKEN SOUP
- 1 CAN CHICKEN GUMBO SOUP
- 1 CAN MUSHROOM BITS AND PIECES
    (DRAINED)
- 1 LARGE CAN DRIED NOODLES
- 2 STALKS CELERY, CHOPPED.
- 1 SMALL ONION (CHOPPED)
- 1½ LBS. GROUND BEEF

BROWN BEEF WITH ONION AND CELERY IN
SMALL AMOUNT OF COOKING OIL. DRAIN.
SPOON INTO LARGE CASSEROLE. ADD ALL
CANNED INGREDIENTS AND MIX THOROUGHLY.
SPRINKLE WITH A FEW DRIED NOODLES.
COOK UNCOVERED FOR ONE HOUR AT 300°
OR UNTIL HEATED THROUGH.

IT'S PERFECTLY SAFE TO SAY YOUR WIFE
IS UNREASONABLE, PROVIDED, OF COURSE,
YOU DO NOT SAY IT TO HER.

SPAGHETTI WITH EGGPLANT SAUCE

½ CUP OLIVE OIL
½ CUP FINELY CHOPPED ONION
2 CLOVES GARLIC, CRUSHED
1 MEDIUM EGGPLANT, PEELED & CUBED
1 CUP SLIVERED GREEN PEPPER
3 CUPS PEELED CHOPPED TOMATOES
½ TSP. DRIED LEAF BASIL
½ TSP. SALT
¼ TSP. PEPPER
½ CUP SLIVERED RIPE OLIVES
1 TBSP. CHOPPED CAPERS
COOKED SPAGHETTI
CHOPPED PARSLEY
PARMESAN CHEESE

HEAT OIL IN HEAVY POT. ADD ONION AND GARLIC AND COOK GENTLY, STIRRING OFTEN, FOR 10 MINUTES. ADD EGGPLANT AND GREEN PEPPER AND CONTINUE COOKING FOR 5 MINUTES, STIRRING CONSTANTLY. ADD TOMATOES, BASIL, SALT AND PEPPER. COVER AND SIMMER 30 MINUTES, STIRRING OCCASIONALLY. ADD OLIVES AND CAPERS. COOK 5 MINUTES MORE.

SERVE OVER BUTTERED SPAGHETTI (WITH MEATBALLS IF DESIRED) GARNISH WITH CHOPPED PARSLEY AND PARMESAN CHEESE.

VEGETABLE SALAD PLATTER

THIS SALAD IS A REAL DELIGHT AND MAY BE SERVED WITH CRAB FILLED BUNS OR AS A BUFFET SALAD. THE LADIES WILL LOVE YOU FOR THIS LOW CALORIE DISH.

- 1 TO 2 HEADS CAULIFLOWER
- 1 TO 2 BASKETS CHERRY TOMATOES
- 1 BUNCH BROCCOLI, WITH STEMS
- 3 TO 4 CARROTS, CUT IN SMALL STRIPS
- 1 BUNCH CHOPPED GREEN ONIONS
- 2 TO 3 STALKS OF CELERY
- 2 CANS BUTTON MUSHROOMS
- 1 8OZ. BOTTLE ITALIAN DRESSING
- PITTED BLACK OLIVES, DRAINED

PREPARE ALL VEGETABLES, CUTTING INTO BITE SIZE PIECES. CHERRY TOMATOES SHOULD BE LEFT WHOLE. PUT ALL INGREDIENTS IN SEALED PLASTIC BOWL OR DOUBLE PLASTIC BAG. POUR DRESSING OVER TO COVER ALL VEGETABLES. MARINATE AND REFRIGERATE FOR 24 HOURS TURNING FREQUENTLY.

DRAIN THOROUGHLY BEFORE SERVING ON A PLATTER. (SEE PICTURE PAGE 123)

WHAT IS REALLY APPALLING IS THAT IN TWENTY YEARS, THESE WILL BE THE GOOD OLD DAYS.

FRESH SPINACH SALAD

SEE PICTURE PAGE 123

1 GARLIC CLOVE, HALVED

2 TBSPS. CIDER OR RED WINE VINEGAR

1 TSP. SUGAR

1 TSP. SALT

1 TSP. DRY MUSTARD

½ TSP. PEPPER (SEASONED PREFERRED)

6 TBSPS. SALAD OIL

8 CUPS CRISP YOUNG SPINACH, HARD STEMS REMOVED (2 TO 2½ LBS.)

3 HARD COOKED EGGS, GRATED

8 SLICES BACON, FRIED AND CRUMBLED

2 OR 3 GREEN ONIONS, CHOPPED FINE

FRESH MUSHROOMS, SLICED "T-" SHAPED

FRESH CAULIFLOWER, SLICED "T-" SHAPED

BEAT FIRST 7 INGREDIENTS AND REFRIGERATE. PREPARE REMAINING INGREDIENTS, ADD DRESSING JUST BEFORE SERVING, REMOVING GARLIC.

FOR VARIATION SEE NEXT PAGE; 'WILTED SPINACH SALAD.'

THE GOOD THING ABOUT SPOILED CHILDREN IS THAT YOU NEVER HAVE ANY IN YOUR OWN FAMILY.

WILTED SPINACH SALAD

- 8 SLICES BACON
- 2 TBSPS. BACON DRIPPINGS
- 8 CUPS SPINACH, HARD STEMS REMOVED
- 3 HARD COOKED EGGS, GRATED
- 2 CHOPPED GREEN ONIONS

COOK BACON, DRAIN AND CRUMBLE. HEAT DRIPPINGS AND ADD DRESSING AS PER 'FRESH SPINACH SALAD' RECIPE, ALONG WITH BACON. POUR DRESSING WHILE HOT OVER SALAD GREENS AND SERVE AT ONCE ON INDIVIDUAL SERVING PLATES.

HORSERADISH SALAD

- 1 PKG. LEMON JELLO
- 1 CUP BOILING WATER
- 1 TSP. SALT
- 2 TBSPS. VINEGAR
- 1 SMALL BOTTLE HORSERADISH, DRAINED
- 1 CUP WHIPPING CREAM, WHIPPED

MIX ALL BUT WHIPPED CREAM AND LET COOL UNTIL JELLO IS PARTIALLY SET. FOLD IN WHIPPED CREAM. THIS IS DELICIOUS WITH ROAST OR BAR-B-QUED BEEF.

MARINATED TOMATOES

1 CAN MUSHROOMS, (OR FRESH)
3 TBSPS. GREEN ONIONS
5 LARGE TOMATOES, SLICED

MARINADE:

1 TSP. CURRY
1 TSP. SUGAR
½ CUP SALAD OIL
¼ CUP VINEGAR
1 CRUSHED GARLIC CLOVE
1 TBSP. PARSLEY
SALT AND PEPPER

COMBINE ALL MARINADE INGREDIENTS IN JAR AND SHAKE WELL. MARINATE VEGETABLES FOR SEVERAL HOURS BEFORE SERVING. ARRANGE ON BED OF LETTUCE IN LARGE OR INDIVIDUAL BOWLS. (SEE PICTURE) PAGE 123.

THE HAPPIEST FAMILIES ARE THOSE IN WHICH THE CHILDREN ARE PROPERLY SPACED. ABOUT TEN FEET APART.

POPPY-SEED SALAD DRESSING

- ⅓ CUP VINEGAR
- ¼ CUP LIME JUICE
- ¾ CUP SUGAR
- 1 TSP. SALT
- ½ TSP. ONION JUICE
- 1 TSP. POPPY SEED
- 1 TSP. DRY MUSTARD
- 1 TSP. PAPRIKA
- 1 CUP SALAD OIL

COMBINE VINEGAR AND LIME JUICE IN PAN, BRING TO BOIL, THEN ADD ALL OTHER INGREDIENTS BUT OIL AND ONION JUICE, STIRRING TO DISSOLVE. ADD OIL AND JUICE, BEAT UNTIL THICKENED. COVER AND CHILL. SERVE ON FRESH FRUIT SALAD, EITHER AS FIRST COURSE OR DESSERT.
(SEE PICTURE) PAGE 17

LADIES — STAY SINGLE. WHO NEEDS A HUSBAND? GET A DOG THAT GROWLS, AND SLEEPS ALL DAY, A PARROT THAT SWEARS AND A CAT THAT STAYS OUT ALL NIGHT.

Frosted Waldorf Salad

2 CUPS MINIATURE MARSHMALLOWS

3 OR 4 CUPS GREEN GRAPES, SEEDLESS
    IF AVAILABLE, IF NOT, REMOVE SEEDS

2 OR 3 UNPEELED CHOPPED RED APPLES

1 PEELED ORANGE, OR
    1 CAN MANDARIN ORANGES, DRAINED
    (RESERVE JUICE TO COAT APPLES)

1 TBSP. ORANGE JUICE

TOSS TOGETHER TO PREVENT APPLES
FROM DISCOLOURING, THEN ADD;

    ½ CUP CHOPPED CELERY

    ½ CUP CHOPPED WALNUTS OR PECANS

    ½ CUP SEEDLESS RAISINS,
        OR SNIPPED DATES (OPTIONAL)

IN A BOWL COMBINE;

    1 CUP WHIPPING CREAM, WHIPPED
        OR WHIPPED TOPPING

    ½ CUP MAYONNAISE

    1 TBSP. SUGAR

COMBINE ALL INGREDIENTS. SERVE IN
LETTUCE LINED GLASS BOWL OR ON
INDIVIDUAL SERVING PLATES, ALONG WITH
WARM BUTTERED ROLLS. GARNISH WITH
ADDITIONAL GREEN GRAPE CLUSTERS,
WASHED AND WHILE DAMP, DIP IN
GRANULATED SUGAR.

CAESAR SALAD

THIS IS A REALLY 'PROFESSIONAL' TASTING
CAESAR BECAUSE YOU MUST DO EVERYTHING
FROM SCRATCH. WITH THE EXCEPTION OF
THE FINAL MIXING, THIS CAN BE DONE
AHEAD OF TIME. THE ONLY EXCEPTION TO
THE INGREDIENTS LISTED IS THAT ON
OCCASION I USE PREPARED CROUTONS,
CATHERINE CLARKE'S BROWNBERRY OVENS
SEASONED CROUTONS BEING THE BEST THAT
I HAVE FOUND.

- 1 LARGE HEAD ROMAINE LETTUCE
- 1 CLOVE GARLIC, HALVED
- ½ CUP SALAD OIL (USE PEANUT, CORN
  OR OLIVE OIL)
- 1 CUP FRENCH BREAD CUBES,
  ½", CRUSTS REMOVED.
- ¾ TSP. SALT
- ¼ TSP. FRESHLY GROUND BLACK PEPPER
- ¼ TSP. DRY MUSTARD
- 1½ TSP. WORCESTERSHIRE SAUCE
- 3 ANCHOVIES, DRAINED AND CHOPPED
- 1 EGG
- 2 TBSPS. GRATED PARMESAN CHEESE
- JUICE OF HALF A LEMON (2 TBSPS)

SEE NEXT PAGE FOR PUTTING
IT TOGETHER!

CONTINUED!

PREPARE ROMAINE LETTUCE BY WASHING AND DRYING THOROUGHLY AND PLACING SEPARATED LEAVES IN PLASTIC BAG AND STORING IN REFRIGERATOR FOR SEVERAL HOURS. BE SURE YOU HAVE TRIMMED THE CORE AND DISCARDED ANY WILTED OR DISCOLOURED LEAVES. SEVERAL HOURS BEFORE SERVING, CRUSH HALF A GARLIC CLOVE AND COMBINE WITH OIL IN JAR WITH TIGHT FITTING LID. REFRIGERATE AT LEAST ONE HOUR. HEAT 2 TBSPS. OIL-GARLIC MIXTURE IN SKILLET. ADD BREAD CUBES, SAUTÉ UNTIL BROWN ALL OVER. SET ASIDE. TO REMAINING OIL-GARLIC MIXTURE IN JAR, ADD SALT, MUSTARD, PEPPER, WORCESTER AND CHOPPED ANCHOVIES. SHAKE VIGOROUSLY. REFRIGERATE. IN A SMALL SAUCEPAN, BRING 2" DEPTH OF WATER TO BOILING. TURN OFF HEAT. CAREFULLY LOWER EGG INTO WATER. LET STAND 1 MINUTE, THEN LIFT OUT. SET ASIDE TO COOL. JUST BEFORE SERVING, RUB THE INSIDE OF A LARGE WOODEN BOWL WITH OTHER HALF OF GARLIC CLOVE. DISCARD THE GARLIC. CUT OUT COARSE RIBS FROM LARGE LEAVES OF ROMAINE. TEAR IN BITESIZE PIECES INTO SALAD BOWL. SHAKE DRESSING AND POUR OVER LETTUCE.

CONTINUED NEXT PAGE!

PICTURED FROM TOP TO BOTTOM: ON PAGE 123
FRESH SPINACH SALAD — PAGE 116
MARINATED VEGETABLE PLATTER - PAGE 115
MARINATED TOMATOES - PAGE 118

CAESAR SALAD

CONTINUED!

Sprinkle lettuce with parmesan. Toss until all leaves are coated with dressing. Break egg over centre of salad (I only use the yolk). Pour lemon juice directly over egg; toss well. Sprinkle with croutons and toss quickly again. Serve at once.

PINK FROSTY SALAD

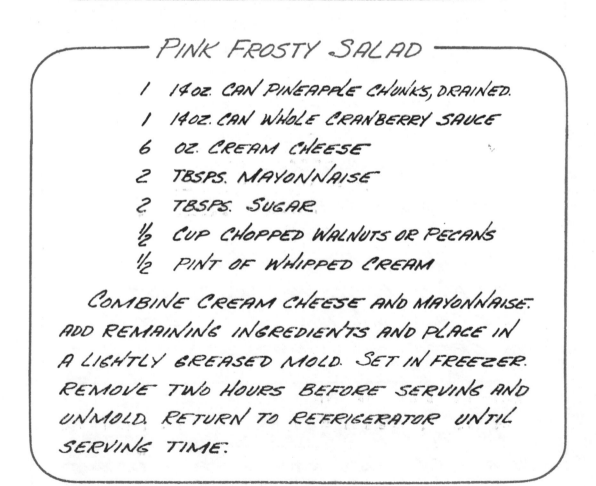

1   14 oz. can pineapple chunks, drained.
1   14 oz. can whole cranberry sauce
6   oz. cream cheese
2   tbsps. mayonnaise
2   tbsps. sugar
½   cup chopped walnuts or pecans
½   pint of whipped cream

Combine cream cheese and mayonnaise. Add remaining ingredients and place in a lightly greased mold. Set in freezer. Remove two hours before serving and unmold. Return to refrigerator until serving time.

SUPER SALAD

1	HEAD ROMAINE LETTUCE
1	HEAD BUTTER LETTUCE
1	HEAD ICEBERG LETTUCE
½	CUP PARMESAN CHEESE
2	OZ. BLUE CHEESE, CRUMBLED
3	AVOCADOS
1	LARGE CUCUMBER, PEELED AND DICED
1½	CUPS CHERRY TOMATOES, HALVED
6	SLICES OF BACON, DRAINED AND CRUMBLED.

SLICED RED AND GREEN PEPPERS, (OPTIONAL)

½	CUP SLICED RIPE OLIVES
1	BOTTLE ITALIAN DRESSING

SPRINKLE PARSLEY

TEAR SALAD GREENS INTO LARGE BOWL, SPRINKLE WITH CHEESE. ARRANGE REMAINING INGREDIENTS ON TOP AND TOSS WITH DRESSING. THIS MAKES A HUGE SALAD AND WILL SERVE 12 TO 14. IT'S GREAT FOR BUFFETS OR BAR-B-QUES.

AN APPLE A DAY KEEPS THE DOCTOR AWAY; AN ONION A DAY KEEPS EVERYONE.

AVOCADO FRUIT SALAD

 2   AVOCADOS, PEELED, SLICED
 2   GRAPEFRUIT, PEELED, CLEANED,
         AND SECTIONED
 2   ORANGES, PEELED, CLEANED,
         AND SECTIONED
 ¼ CUP LEMON JUICE
 LETTUCE, ROMAINE OR BUTTER
 WATERCRESS (OPTIONAL)

DIP AVOCADO IN LEMON JUICE (RESERVE JUICE).
ARRANGE FRUIT WITH LETTUCE. ADD
WATERCRESS. SPOON DRESSING OVER ALL.

DRESSING

 ⅓ CUP CITRUS JUICE (USE LEMON JUICE
         FROM DIPPING AVOCADO. ADD JUICE
         FROM FRUIT SECTIONS)
 1   CUP SALAD OIL
 ½ CUP SUGAR
 1   TSP. SALT
 1   TSP. GRATED ONION
 1½ TBSPS. POPPY SEEDS
 ½ TSP. DRY MUSTARD

SHAKE ALL INGREDIENTS TOGETHER
UNTIL WELL BLENDED.

PINEAPPLE COLESLAW

1   MEDIUM CABBAGE
2   14 OZ. CANS PINEAPPLE TIDBITS
1   TBSP. LEMON JUICE
3   RED APPLES
¾   CUP SLICED ALMONDS

FINELY SHRED CABBAGE. DICE APPLES AND SPRINKLE WITH LEMON JUICE TO AVOID DISCOLOURING. ADD PINEAPPLE AND ALMONDS.

DRESSING

½   CUP MAYONNAISE
½   CUP HEAVY CREAM, WHIPPED
½   CUP LEMONADE CONCENTRATE

COMBINE MAYONNAISE AND LEMONADE. ADD TO CREAM AND MIX THOROUGHLY WITH SALAD INGREDIENTS.

THE TROUBLE WITH THE WORLD TODAY IS THAT EVERY DAY BEGINS WITH THE FIRST HALF HOUR.

HAMBURGER SOUP

DON'T BE DECEIVED BY THE NAME—THIS IS A FAMILY FAVORITE AND GREAT FOR ENTERTAINING. THIS RECIPE MAKES 18 SOUP LADLES AND IT FREEZES VERY WELL.

- 1½ LBS. GROUND BEEF
- 1 MEDIUM ONION (CHOPPED FINE)
- 1 28 OZ. CAN TOMATOES
- 2 CUPS WATER
- 3 CANS CONSOMMÉ
- 1 CAN TOMATO SOUP
- 4 CARROTS (CHOPPED FINE)
- 1 BAY LEAF
- 3 STICKS CELERY (CHOPPED FINE)
- PARSLEY
- ½ TSP. THYME
- PEPPER TO TASTE
- 8 TBSPS. BARLEY

BROWN MEAT AND ONIONS. DRAIN WELL. COMBINE ALL INGREDIENTS IN LARGE POT. SIMMER COVERED, AT LEAST 2 HOURS, OR ALL DAY. SERVES 10.

IF AT FIRST YOU DON'T SUCCEED.... WELL SO MUCH FOR SKY DIVING.

GAZPACHO

SERVES 8

- 3 LBS. (6 CUPS) FRESH TOMATOES PEELED AND CUT UP.
- 1 ONION - CUT IN CHUNKS
- ½ CUP GREEN PEPPER CHUNKS
- ½ CUP CUCUMBER CHUNKS
- 2 CUPS TOMATO JUICE
- 1 CLOVE GARLIC MINCED
- ½ TSP. CUMIN
- 1 TSP. SALT
- 1 TSP. PEPPER
- ¼ CUP OLIVE OIL
- ¼ CUP WHITE WINE VINEGAR

BLANCH TOMATOES TO PEEL. IN BLENDER COMBINE THE FIRST FOUR INGREDIENTS AND TRANSFER TO LARGE TUREEN. ADD JUICE, GARLIC, CUMIN, SALT AND PEPPER. COVER AND CHILL WELL. BEFORE SERVING, STIR IN OIL AND VINEGAR. SERVE COLD.

GARNISH

- ½ CUP FINELY CHOPPED GREEN ONION
- ½ CUP FINELY CHOPPED GREEN PEPPER
- ½ CUP CROUTONS.

Grampa Mac's Oyster Stew

This very rich soup recipe comes from a grandfather from P.E.I. Serves four hungry people — a meal by itself served with toast and cheese.

- 2 5oz. cans oysters, with liquid
- 1/3 cup butter
- 3/4 tsp. salt
- 1/8 tsp. Worcestershire sauce
- Pepper to taste
- 1 16oz. can evaporated milk
- 2/3 cup regular milk
- 12 single soda crackers

Heat everything except milk and crackers over medium heat to a near boil. Add evaporated milk and continue stirring over heat. Break soda crackers on top and stir. Add remaining milk being careful not to boil. Serve.

Marriage is like a cafeteria; you take what looks good to you, and pay for it later.

CHILI SAUCE

- 1 28 OZ. TIN TOMATOES
- 1 CUP BROWN SUGAR
- 1 CUP VINEGAR
- 1 LARGE CHOPPED ONION
- 1 TSP. CINNAMON
- 1 TSP. ALLSPICE

SPRINKLE OF GINGER
CHILI PEPPERS

THESE INGREDIENTS ARE COOKED TOGETHER UNTIL THE MIXTURE THICKENS AND BECOMES A DARK RED. THIS WILL TAKE PRETTY WELL THE WHOLE DAY AT A LOW HEAT. STIR OCCASIONALLY. THE TOMATOES SHOULD BE CUT UP. USE YOUR DISCRETION WITH THE CHILI PEPPERS. USE THE BOTTLED CRUSHED CHILIES FROM THE SPICE SECTION. I KEEP TASTING IT THROUGH THE DAY AND ADD MORE UNTIL IT IS AS HOT AS I WANT IT. THIS IS A NICE CONDIMENT WITH ANY BEEF OR MACARONI DISH.

MISERY IS THE INABILITY TO CONCEAL THE FACT THAT YOU'VE HAD A FOURTH MARTINI.

GREEN TOMATO RELISH

7½ LBS. GREEN TOMATOES - UNRIPENED.
4   LARGE ONIONS
1   CUP SALT
1   QT. VINEGAR
6   CUPS SUGAR
5   GREEN PEPPERS
4   RED PEPPERS
1   TSP. CINNAMON
1   TSP. CLOVES
1   TBSP. TUMERIC
2   TBSPS. MIXED PICKLING SPICES.

SLICE TOMATOES, PEPPERS AND ONIONS. COVER WITH SALT AND LET STAND OVERNIGHT. RINSE OFF SALT.

PUT ALL IN LARGE POT AND COOK UNTIL DESIRED CONSISTENCY. PUT IN STERILIZED JARS AND SEAL.

DELICIOUS SERVED WITH ROAST BEEF.

MAN WILL NEVER FEEL LONELY EATING SPAGHETTI.....THERE'S TOO MUCH TO DO.

30	RIPE TOMATOES
6	PEACHES
6	PEARS
4	ONIONS
3	TBSPS. SALT
2	RED PEPPERS
2	GREEN PEPPERS
4	CUPS VINEGAR
4	CUPS BROWN SUGAR
2	TSPS. WHOLE CLOVES
2	TSPS. STICK CINNAMON

(WRAP IN CHEESECLOTH)

SCALD, PEEL AND CHOP TOMATOES, PEACHES, PEARS AND ONIONS. MIX WITH OTHER INGREDIENTS, (EXCEPT SPICES). SIMMER TWO (2) HOURS. ADD SPICES DURING LAST 15 MINUTES. REMOVE SPICES AND PUT IN STERILIZED JARS - SEAL.

THIS YIELDS 5 TO 6 QUARTS. DELICIOUS SERVED WITH ANY MEAT. PLACE THIS ON YOUR BUFFET WHEN HAVING - "MAKE YOUR OWN SANDWICHES"

TERIYAKI SAUCE FOR STEAK

BLEND THE FOLLOWING IN OSTERIZER;

1	ONION
2	CLOVES GARLIC
2	TSPS. GINGER
½	FRESH MASHED PAPAYA (OPTIONAL)
½	CUP WATER

ADD;

2½	TBSPS. BROWN SUGAR
25	OZ. SOY SAUCE
12	OZ. WATER

STORE IN REFRIGERATOR INDEFINITELY. FOR FLANK STEAK OR THE CHEAPER CUTS OF MEAT, MARINATE FOR 24 HOURS. USE ON CHICKEN AND ANY STEAKS.

GINGER SOY SAUCE FOR BEEF

½	CUP SOY SAUCE
1	TSP. GROUND GINGER

MIX TOGETHER AND BRING TO BOIL.

THIS IS A MARVELLOUS DIP FOR FONDUE, OR EVEN IN PLACE OF WORCESTERSHIRE WITH STEAK. FOR ORIENTAL STIR-FRIED DINNERS, PLACE INDIVIDUAL SAUCE DISHES AT EACH PLACE.

CRANBERRY BURGUNDY SAUCE

This is a delicious change for a glazed ham or chicken glaze.

- 1 large can cranberry sauce
- 1 cup brown sugar
- ½ cup burgundy (dry red wine)
- 2 tsp. prepared mustard

Mix ingredients in saucepan and heat to boiling. Stir until sugar has dissolved. Spoon over ham or chicken while they cook and use remaining sauce for accompanying the dinner.

If looks could kill, a lot of people would die with bridge cards in their hands.

MUSTARD SAUCE FOR HAM

- 2 egg yolks
- ½ cup sugar
- 2 dessert spoons, dry mustard
- ⅓ cup white vinegar

Combine ingredients and bring to boil. Ideal for serving with ham for a buffet; either for hot ham or for sandwiches.

III GOODIES

Forgotten Cookies

(SEE PICTURE PAGE 141)

2 EGG WHITES
3/4 CUP SUGAR
1/2 TSP. VANILLA
6 OZ. SEMI-SWEET CHOCOLATE CHIPS
1 CUP CHOPPED PECANS

PREHEAT OVEN TO 350°. BEAT EGG WHITES UNTIL STIFF, ADD SUGAR GRADUALLY. BEAT AT HIGH SPEED 5 MINUTES. FOLD IN VANILLA, CHIPS AND PECANS. DROP FROM TEASPOON ONTO FOIL-LINED COOKIE SHEET. PUT IN OVEN AND TURN OFF HEAT. LEAVE OVERNIGHT OR AT LEAST 8 HOURS. MAKES ABOUT 3 DOZEN MERINGUE-LIKE COOKIES. YOU CAN ADD A FEW DROPS OF FOOD COLOURING (WITH NUTS AND CHIPS) IF YOU WANT THEM COLOURED.

IF WE COULD TRAIN OURSELVES TO BREATHE THROUGH OUR EARS, WE COULD PUT OUR FACES RIGHT DOWN INTO THE SOUP AND NOT REQUIRE SPOONS.

PECAN MACAROONS

This is a pretty Christmas cookie and is good too! (See picture page 141.)

- ½ cup white sugar
- ¼ cup boiling water
- 1 egg white
- ½ cup brown sugar
- 1½ cups coconut
- 2 tbsps. caramel syrup (see below)
- ½ cups glace cherries, whole
- 1 cup whole pecans

TO MAKE CARAMEL SYRUP:

Melt ½ cup of white sugar in pot over medium heat. CAREFULLY add ¼ cup boiling water. (Mixture of hot sugar and water can 'explode' if not added away from heat and with caution!) Sugar will harden, but the liquid will make at least 2 tbsps. syrup. Cool completely!

COOKIES:

Beat egg whites, adding pinch of salt. Add additional ingredients and 2 tbsps. cooled syrup. Bake at 325° for 15 minutes or until lightly browned. Cookies will slightly run together on sheet; therefore, while still hot, push cookie back together with a spoon. Cool on cookie sheet. Makes approximately 3 dozen cookies.

PICTURED FROM TOP TO BOTTOM:
EGGNOG SUPREME   PAGE 59
ROLLED ASPARAGUS SANDWICHES PAGE 28

<u>CENTRE TRAY</u> (CLOCKWISE FROM TOP)
PECAN MACAROONS   PAGE 140
FORGOTTEN COOKIES PAGE 139
VERNA'S CHOCOLATE SQUARE PAGE 201
WHIPPED SHORTBREAD   PAGE 146
CHRISTMAS CAKE PAGE 202

<u>LOWER TRAY</u> (CLOCKWISE FROM TOP)
SNOWBALLS   PAGE 148
MAGIC COOKIE BARS PAGE 196
DREAM SLICE PAGE 194
SWEDISH PASTRY   PAGE 143
SHORTBREAD TARTS WITH MINCEMEAT OR...
...LEMON FILLING PAGE 199
JEWISH SHORTBREAD PAGE 145
GEORGE PAGE 198

SWEDISH PASTRY

(SEE PICTURE PAGE 141)

½ CUP BUTTER
¼ CUP BROWN SUGAR
1 CUP FLOUR (OR ENOUGH TO MAKE
A COOKIE DOUGH)
1 EGG, SEPARATED
PINCH OF SALT

MIX TOGETHER, RESERVING EGG WHITE, AND ROLL INTO BALLS. DIP IN SLIGHTLY BEATEN EGG WHITE AND ROLL IN CRUSHED WALNUTS. PLACE ON A GREASED PAN. PRESS IN CENTRE WITH A THIMBLE. BAKE AT 325° FOR A FEW MINUTES, THEN REMOVE FROM OVEN AND PRESS WITH THIMBLE AGAIN. RETURN TO OVEN AND BAKE UNTIL NICELY BROWNED. FILL CENTRES WITH JAM OR HALF A CHERRY.

PRALINES

3 TBSPS. MELTED BUTTER
1 CUP BROWN SUGAR
1 EGG
4 TBSPS. FLOUR
1 CUP PECANS, CHOPPED
1 TSP. VANILLA

MIX ALL INGREDIENTS WELL AND DROP WITH SMALL TEASPOON ONTO GREASED SHEET. BAKE 5 MINUTES AT 350°. REMOVE IMMEDIATELY.

MONA'S MOTHER'S MOTHER'S BEST FRIEND'S FAVORITE

THIS IS A VERY OLD RECIPE!

- 1 CUP WHITE SUGAR
- ½ CUP BROWN SUGAR
- X EGG
- 1 CUP BUTTER
- 1¼ CUP FLOUR
- 1¼ CUPS ROLLED QUICK OATS
- ¾ CUP COCONUT
- 1 TSP. BAKING POWDER
- 1 TSP. BAKING SODA

IN MEDIUM BOWL, BEAT EGG. ADD BUTTER, BROWN AND WHITE SUGAR. CREAM WELL. ADD REMAINING INGREDIENTS. BAKE AT 350° FOR 12 TO 15 MINUTES OR UNTIL GOLDEN. THESE ARE A LIGHT, TASTY COOKIE FOR THE KIDS AND A ONE BOWL MIXTURE - ALWAYS HANDY.

THE YEARS A WOMAN SUBTRACTS FROM HER AGE ARE NOT LOST; THEY ARE ADDED TO THE AGES OF OTHER WOMEN.

JEWISH SHORTBREAD

- ½ LB. SOFT BUTTER
- ⅓ CUP WHITE SUGAR
- ½ CUP FINELY GROUND NUTS
- 1 TSP. VANILLA
- 1⅔ CUPS FLOUR
- PINCH OF SALT
- ½ CUP WHITE SUGAR
- 4 TSP. CINNAMON

MIX FIRST 6 INGREDIENTS TOGETHER—
BEAT WELL. SHAPE INTO CRESCENTS AND
PLACE 1 INCH APART ON UNGREASED COOKIE
SHEET. BAKE AT 325° FOR 15 TO 20
MINUTES. WHILE STILL WARM COAT WITH SUGAR
AND CINNAMON. FOR VARIETY COAT WITH
ICING SUGAR. (SEE PICTURE, PAGE 141)

SHORTBREAD

- 1 LB. BUTTER
- 4 TO 5 CUPS. FLOUR
- 1 CUP BERRY SUGAR

CREAM BUTTER WITH SUGAR. ADD FLOUR,
BEATING FOR FIVE MINUTES. ROLL OUT DOUGH
AND USE COOKIE CUTTERS. BAKE AT 300° FOR
10 TO 15 MINUTES OR UNTIL LIGHTLY GOLDEN.

CHEESE SHORTBREAD

½ LB. McLAREN'S IMPERIAL CHEESE
½ LB. BUTTER
2 CUPS FLOUR
2 TBSPS. LIGHT BROWN SUGAR

MIX INGREDIENTS TOGETHER AND KNEAD. FORM INTO A ROLL. SLICE THIN AND BAKE AT 250° TO 275° FOR 1 HOUR.

THESE ARE PARTICULARLY GOOD TO SERVE WITH DRINKS.

OF COURSE THERE'S SUCH A THING AS LUCK- HOW ELSE COULD YOU EXPLAIN YOUR ENEMIES SUCCESSES.

WHIPPED SHORTBREAD

THESE MELT IN YOUR MOUTH. THE SECRET IS IN THE BEATING.

1 CUP BUTTER
1½ CUPS FLOUR
½ CUP ICING SUGAR

COMBINE ALL INGREDIENTS AND BEAT FOR 10 MINUTES. DROP FROM TEASPOON ONTO COOKIE SHEET. DECORATE WITH MARASCHINO CHERRY PIECES. BAKE AT 350° FOR APPROXIMATELY 17 MINUTES UNTIL BOTTOMS ARE LIGHTLY BROWNED. MAKES APPROXIMATELY 3 DOZEN SMALL COOKIES. (SEE PICTURE PAGE 141)

SOFT RAISIN COOKIES

3 CUPS SEEDLESS RAISINS
1½ TSP. CINNAMON
1½ TSP. NUTMEG
1½ TSP. GINGER
½ CUP SHORTENING
1½ CUPS WHITE SUGAR
2 EGGS
2 TSP. SODA
1 TSP. SALT
3½ CUPS FLOUR

PLACE RAISINS AND SPICES IN SAUCEPAN AND COVER WITH WATER TO 1 INCH ABOVE RAISINS. COOK ABOUT 20 MINUTES UNCOVERED OR UNTIL WATER IS REDUCED TO LEVEL OF RAISINS. COOL SLIGHTLY. COMBINE THE REMAINING INGREDIENTS. MIXTURE WILL BE DRY AND MEALY BUT DO NOT DESPAIR, ADD RAISIN MIXTURE AND YOU'RE THERE! (IF TOO DRY, ADD ADDITIONAL WATER CAREFULLY.) DROP FROM DESSERT SPOON ONTO COOKIE SHEET. MAKES APPROXIMATELY 48 LARGE COOKIES. BAKE AT 350° FOR 15 TO 20 MINUTES.

BACHELORS ARE LIKE DETERGENTS; BOTH WORK FAST AND LEAVE NO RINGS.

SNOWBALLS

⅞ CUP FLOUR
½ CUP BUTTER (NOT MARGARINE)
1 TBSP. SUGAR
PINCH OF SALT
1 TSP. VANILLA
1 CUP FINELY GROUND PECANS
   (BE SURE THEY ARE FRESH)
1 CUP ICING SUGAR

CREAM BUTTER AND SUGAR. ADD NUTS AND VANILLA. WORK IN FLOUR, BLEND WELL. FORM SMALL BALLS AND BAKE ON UNGREASED SHEET AT 300° FOR 8 TO 10 MINUTES. UNTIL BARELY BROWN. COAT THOROUGHLY IN ICING SUGAR WHILE HOT. (SEE PICTURE PAGE 141.)

CHOCOLATE SNOWBALLS

9 SQUARES SEMI-SWEET CHOCOLATE
1 TIN EAGLE BRAND MILK
1 CUP WALNUTS, PECANS OR ALMONDS
SHREDDED COCONUT

MELT CHOCOLATE, ADD MILK AND NUTS. COOK APPROXIMATELY ½ HOUR STIRRING OCCASIONALLY. ROLL INTO BALLS AND ROLL IN COCONUT. REFRIGERATE.

CANDIED ALMONDS

¼ CUP WATER
½ CUP SUGAR
1 CUP ALMONDS (OR PECANS)

PLACE INGREDIENTS IN CAST IRON FRYING PAN. (THIS RECIPE DOUBLED FITS WELL INTO A 10 INCH PAN.)

COOK ABOUT 10 MINUTES STIRRING CONSTANTLY WITH WOODEN SPOON. MIXTURE WILL BECOME POWDERY WHITE, THEN GLAZE WILL BEGIN.

KEEP STIRRING UNTIL NUTS ARE COVERED WITH THE GLAZE. TURN OUT ON BREADBOARD AND SEPARATE — BE CAREFUL AS NUTS ARE VERY HOT.

THESE MAKE NICE CHRISTMAS GIFTS IN LITTLE BOWLS OR JARS.

MIDDLE AGE IS THAT TIME OF LIFE WHEN YOU CAN FEEL BAD IN THE MORNING WITHOUT HAVING HAD FUN THE NIGHT BEFORE.

Chocolate Fudge Balls

3   SQUARES UNSWEETENED CHOCOLATE
3   TBSPS. BUTTER
1/3   CUP MASHED POTATOES
1/8   TSP. SALT
1   TSP. VANILLA
3   CUPS ICING SUGAR
3/4   CUP FINELY CHOPPED WALNUTS
      (COCONUT MAY BE USED)

MELT CHOCOLATE AND BUTTER IN TOP OF DOUBLE BOILER. ADD POTATOES, SALT AND VANILLA. MIX WELL. BLEND IN SUGAR, ONE CUP AT A TIME, THOROUGHLY MIX, AND KNEAD GENTLY. SHAPE INTO SMALL BALLS AND ROLL IN WALNUTS. SET ON WAX PAPER, DRY BEFORE STORING.

BEFORE YOU ACCUSE YOUR HUSBAND OF INFIDELITY... PAUSE TO REFLECT. HE MAY HAVE BEEN FAITHFUL TO YOU DOZENS OF TIMES.

CHEESE CAKE

CRUMB CRUST:

1¾ CUPS GRAHAM WAFER CRUMBS
¼ CUP FINELY CHOPPED WALNUTS
½ TSP. CINNAMON
½ CUP BUTTER

PRESS COMBINED INGREDIENTS INTO SPRING FORM PAN.

3 EGGS
2 8 OZ. PKG. CREAM CHEESE
1 CUP SUGAR
2 TSPS. VANILLA
3 CUPS SOUR CREAM
FRESH STRAWBERRIES

BLEND CHEESE, SUGAR AND EGGS. ADD SOUR CREAM, VANILLA, MIXING WELL, THEN POUR INTO WAFER SHELL. BAKE AT 375° FOR 50 TO 60 MINUTES.

TO SERVE, DECORATE WITH FRESH STRAWBERRIES, OR ANY FRUIT GLAZE.

SOME MEN ARE ATTRACTED BY A GIRL'S MIND. OTHERS ARE ATTRACTED BY WHAT SHE DOESN'T MIND.

ANGEL MOCHA TORTE

MERINGUES:

4 EGG WHITES
1 CUP BROWN SUGAR
1 CUP BLANCHED SLICED ALMONDS
PINCH OF SALT

FILLING:

1/2 PINT WHIPPING CREAM, WHIPPED
1/2 CUP BROWN SUGAR
1 TBSP. INSTANT COFFEE

TOAST ALMONDS-RESERVE HANDFUL FOR DECORATION, CHOP THE REMAINDER.

BEAT EGG WHITES AND SALT UNTIL ALMOST STIFF. ADD SUGAR AND BEAT UNTIL GLOSSY PEAKS ARE FORMED. FOLD IN CHOPPED ALMONDS. HAVE READY FOUR BROWN PAPER CIRCLES, LAYER CAKE PAN SIZE. SPREAD MIXTURE ON CIRCLES, ON COOKIE SHEETS, MAKING EACH 1/2" THICK. ADD RESERVED ALMONDS AS DECORATION ON ONE CIRCLE. BAKE TWO AT A TIME AT 250° FOR ONE HOUR. TURN OFF OVEN AND LEAVE UNTIL DRIED OUT. COOL ON A RACK, PREFERABLY OVERNIGHT, AND GENTLY PEEL OFF PAPER. MERINGUES MUST BE HANDLED VERY CAREFULLY AS THEY WILL BREAK. HOWEVER, BROKEN MERINGUES MAY BE HIDDEN UNDER FILLING.   CONTINUED NEXT PAGE!

ANGEL MOCHA TORTE

CONTINUED!

ADD ½ CUP OF BROWN SUGAR AND INSTANT COFFEE TO WHIPPED CREAM. SPREAD BETWEEN LAYERS, USING DECORATED MERINGUE AS THE TOP. REFRIGERATE 4 HOURS BEFORE SERVING.

THIS RECIPE IS A LOT OF WORK— BUT A GUARANTEED HIT!

A FOOL AND HIS MONEY ARE SOON POPULAR.

RUM CAKE

1 CHIFFON CAKE, READY-MADE
1 CUP MAPLE SYRUP
¼ CUP RUM
SHREDDED COCONUT OR CHOPPED NUTS
WHIPPED CREAM

COMBINE MAPLE SYRUP AND RUM. ROLL CAKE IN SYRUP MIXTURE, THEN IN SHREDDED COCONUT OR CHOPPED NUTS. TOP EACH SERVING WITH WHIPPED CREAM FLAVORED WITH RUM.

This cake is made entirely from mixes which is great for two reasons - it never fails and you can keep the ingredients indefinitely. It also tastes terrific!

* 1   PKG. ANGEL FOOD CAKE MIX
  ½   CUP MILK
  1   PKG. VANILLA PUDDING MIX
      (THE KIND YOU COOK)
  1   PKG. DREAM WHIP & 1½ CUPS MILK
  ½   TSP. ALMOND EXTRACT

TOPPING:

  1   CAN MANDARIN ORANGES - DRAINED
  ½   CUP TOASTED SLIVERED ALMONDS

Preheat oven to 375°. Prepare angel cake mix as directed. Push batter into ungreased pan. You may use either a 9" x 13" pan or a 10" tube pan. (Keep in mind that this cake will really rise during baking and if you have some batter left over, cook it in another pan and use for another dessert.) Cut through batter with a knife to remove air. Spread smooth. Bake on lowest oven rack 30 to 40 minutes. Invert cake to cool. Let hang 2 hours. Cont'd.
(*IF USING 10" TUBE PAN, DOUBLE FILLING RECIPE.)

ANGEL FOOD FLAN

FILLING: *

PREPARE VANILLA PUDDING AS DIRECTED, USING 1½ CUPS MILK. COVER SURFACE OF PUDDING WITH WAX PAPER TO PREVENT SCUM FROM FORMING. CHILL. PREPARE DREAM WHIP AS DIRECTED USING ½ CUP MILK AND ½ TSP. ALMOND FLAVORING. BEAT CHILLED PUDDING UNTIL LIGHT. FOLD IN DREAM WHIP. LOOSEN AND TURN OUT CAKE. IF 9" x 13", CUT IN HALF. IF IN TUBE PAN, CUT INTO TWO LAYERS. SPREAD FILLING BETWEEN LAYERS, RESERVING ENOUGH TO FROST ENTIRE CAKE. DECORATE WITH MANDARIN ORANGES AND TOASTED ALMONDS. (SEE PICTURE) PAGE 171.

* FOR A FIRMER FILLING, ADD ONE TSP. CORN STARCH TO DREAM WHIP. (SEE PICTURE PAGE 175).

A LOSER IS A WINDOW WASHER ON THE 44TH FLOOR WHO STEPS BACK TO ADMIRE HIS WORK!

THE MEN IN YOUR LIFE WILL LOVE THIS.

- 1 CUP BROWN SUGAR
- 1 CUP HOT WATER

COMBINE AND HEAT UNTIL A SYRUP.

- 1 CUP FLOUR
- 2 TSP. BAKING POWDER
- 1/2 TSP. SALT
- 2 TBSPS. SHORTENING
- 1/3 CUP MILK

MIX AND ROLL INTO RECTANGULAR SHAPE.

- 2 APPLES, PEELED AND SLICED
- DASH BROWN SUGAR
- DASH CINNAMON
- WHIPPING CREAM, WHIPPED

SPRINKLE PASTRY WITH SUGAR AND CINNAMON. SPREAD APPLES ON TOP. ROLL UP AND SLICE 1" THICK. PUT CUT SIDE DOWN IN BAKING DISH. DOT WITH BUTTER AND POUR SYRUP OVER. BAKE IN 350° OVEN FOR 30 MINUTES OR UNTIL BROWN ON TOP. SERVE WITH WHIPPED CREAM.

'A GOSSIP'- THE KNIFE OF THE PARTY.

CHOCOLATE MINT PIE

9" CRUMB PIE SHELL
2 SQ. SEMI-SWEET CHOCOLATE
1 CUP ICING SUGAR
¼ LB. BUTTER
2 EGGS
1 TSP. VANILLA
1 TSP. PEPPERMINT
WHIPPED CREAM
CHOCOLATE CURLS

CREAM BUTTER AND SUGAR. MELT CHOCOLATE SLOWLY OVER LOW HEAT. ADD CHOCOLATE, BEATEN EGGS TO BUTTER MIXTURE AND BEAT AT HIGH SPEED UNTIL FLUFFY. ADD VANILLA AND PEPPERMINT. POUR INTO COOLED SHELL. REFRIGERATE FOR 24 HOURS BEFORE SERVING. SERVE WITH WHIPPED CREAM AND GARNISH WITH CHOCOLATE CURLS.

THE DIFFERENCE BETWEEN A STOIC AND A CYNIC IS; THE STOIC IS WHAT BRINGS THE KID AND A CYNIC IS WHAT YOU WASHES HIM IN!

BRANDY SNAPS

A fussy hour of preparing the shells will provide you with a top-notch company dessert, which may be prepared and frozen days in advance.

- ½ cup butter
- ½ cup sugar
- ⅓ cup dark molasses
- ½ cup flour
- Pinch of salt
- 1 tsp. ground ginger
- 1 tsp. lemon juice
- ½ tsp. vanilla

Have ready rolling pin, broom handle or long empty cardboard gift wrap tube or tin foil tubes. Set oven at 350°. Melt the butter, sugar and molasses in a pan, stirring until the butter is melted. Cool slightly. Sift flour, salt and ginger into the butter mixture, stirring well, and adding lemon juice and vanilla last. Cool. Onto a well greased cookie sheet, drop the mixture half a teaspoon at a time, allowing only 5 or 6 to each large cookie sheet. These will spread on the sheet during baking into thin wafers ideally 3" to 4" in diameter. Cont'd. next page

Bake for 7 or 8 minutes, or until each wafer bubbles all over and is browned. Immediately separate wafers with a spatula and cool for ½ a minute. Working rapidly, remove from cookie sheet and roll and shape, bubbled side out, around broom handle, cardboard tubing or any similar object. Allow to cool in this position until it will remain in rolled position. You may find it preferable to leave the shell partially open so that it is easier to fill. If they harden before they are rolled, return to the oven for a few moments.

These shells may be frozen at this point and filled just before serving with whipped cream laced with brandy. Or... slightly thaw vanilla ice cream, add ¼ to ½ cup brandy, and whip till smooth. Freeze. After shells have cooled completely, fill each with the brandied ice cream and return to freezer until serving time. To serve, arrange on serving plate, garnish each with brandied whipped cream and nuts. For the final touch, warm some brandy, and at the table, pour over all brandy snaps and flame.

FRUIT COCKTAIL CAKE

A GREAT LAST MINUTE DESSERT —
SUPER EASY. YOUR FAMILY AND YOUR COMPANY
WILL LOVE IT.

- 1½ CUPS WHITE SUGAR
- 2 CUPS FLOUR
- 2 TSPS. BAKING SODA
- ½ TSP. SALT
- 2 EGGS
- 14 OZ. CAN FRUIT COCKTAIL WITH JUICE
  (OR TINNED PINEAPPLE)

BEAT EGGS SLIGHTLY. ADD ALL INGREDIENTS
EXCEPT FLOUR. ADD FLOUR AND BAKE IN
9" x 13" PAN (GREASED) FOR 45 MINUTES
AT 350°

ICING :

- ¾ CUP WHITE SUGAR
- ½ CUP CREAM (MILK WILL DO)
- ½ CUP BUTTER
- 1 TSP. VANILLA (1 TSP. BRANDY
  IS A SUPERB SUBSTITUTE!)

BOIL ALL INGREDIENTS EXCEPT VANILLA.
ADD VANILLA AND POUR OVER HOT CAKE.
(MAKES A LOT, BUT USE ALL OF IT!)
N.B. SERVE WARM WITH WHIPPED CREAM
OR VANILLA ICE CREAM. KEEPS REFRIGERATED
FOR SEVERAL DAYS.

COFFEE ICE CREAM PIE

2 OR 3 TBSP. BUTTER
3/4 CUP SHREDDED COCONUT
1/2 QUART COFFEE ICE CREAM,
    SOFTENED.

SPREAD BUTTER EVENLY ON BOTTOM AND SIDES OF 9 INCH PIE PLATE. SPRINKLE SHREDDED COCONUT OVER TOP AND PRESS EVENLY INTO BUTTER. BAKE AT 300° FOR 15 TO 20 MINUTES UNTIL BROWN. COOL. PUT ICE CREAM IN SHELL AND PUT IN FRIG TO SET. TOP WITH BUTTERSCOTCH SAUCE.

SAUCE

1 CUP LIGHT CREAM
2 TBSPS BUTTER
3/4 CUP BROWN SUGAR
1 TBSP. CORN SYRUP

MIX IN HEAVY POT OVER LOW HEAT STIRRING FREQUENTLY UNTIL MIXTURE IS SMOOTH AND THICK. COOL. LIGHTLY BURN SLIVERED ALMONDS IN SMALL AMOUNT OF BUTTER SPRINKLE OVER TOP. THIS MAY BE FROZEN FOR LATER USE. YOU MAY WISH TO TOP WITH WHIPPING CREAM.

SMALL PORTIONS ARE SUFFICIENT!

2½ CUPS GRAHAM WAFER CRUMBS
    (SAVE ½ CUP FOR TOPPING)
½ CUP BUTTER
½ CUP BUTTER
1½ CUPS ICING SUGAR
2 UNBEATEN EGGS
1 14 OZ. TIN CRUSHED PINEAPPLE,
    DRAINED
1 CUP WHIPPING CREAM, WHIPPED

COMBINE WAFER CRUMBS AND ½ CUP BUTTER, PAT INTO 8"×8" SQUARE PAN AND BAKE FOR 10 MINUTES AT 375°, COOL.

CREAM ½ CUP BUTTER WITH ICING SUGAR, AND ADD EGGS ONE AT A TIME, BEATING WELL AFTER EACH ADDITION. SPOON ONTO CRUST. WHIP CREAM, THEN FOLD IN PINEAPPLE. POUR OVER EGG MIXTURE AND SPRINKLE WITH CRUMBS. REFRIGERATE FOR ONE HOUR BEFORE SERVING.

MAY BE SERVED WITH AN EXTRA SPOONFUL OF CRUSHED PINEAPPLE ON EACH SLICE

THERE COMES A TIME IN A MAN'S LIFE WHEN A YEN IS ONLY CHINESE MONEY.

PEACH FLAMBÉ

8 PEACH HALVES, RESERVING JUICE
1 TBSP. BUTTER
JUICE OF 2 ORANGES
3 OZ. BRANDY
1½ OZ. GRAND MARNIER
1½ OZ. SLIVERED ALMONDS
⅓ CUP SUGAR
1½ OZ. KIRSCH
JUICE OF 1 GRAPEFRUIT
JUICE OF 1 LEMON
8 SCOOPS, LEMON SHERBERT

BROWN THE SUGAR, STIRRING CONSTANTLY, UNTIL CARAMELIZED. ADD BUTTER, PEACH JUICE AND LIQUEURS. REMOVE FROM HEAT AND FLAME. ADD JUICES OF LEMON, GRAPEFRUIT AND ORANGES, COOKING FOR ABOUT 3 MINUTES. ADD PEACH HALVES, WARM AND SERVE OVER SHERBERT. SERVES 8.

'TEAKETTLE' - A MARVELLOUS APPLIANCE. I'D LOVE TO SEE YOU SING WITH YOUR NOSE FULL OF BOILING WATER!

CRÈME DE MENTHE DESSERT

- 1 REG. PACKAGE OREO BISCUITS, CRUSHED
- 1 LARGE PACKAGE MARSHMALLOWS
- 1 CUP MILK
- 1 PINT OF WHIPPED CREAM
- 6 TBSPS. CRÈME DE MENTHE

MELT MARSHMALLOWS IN DOUBLE BOILER WITH MILK. COOL. WHIP THE CREAM AND ADD TO COOLED MARSHMALLOWS. FOLD IN CRÈME DE MENTHE.

PLACE HALF OF THE CRUMBS IN A 9"x13" PAN COVER WITH MIXTURE. ADD REMAINDER OF THE CRUMBS TO TOP. REFRIGERATE OVERNIGHT.

YOU MAY ALSO USE CRUSHED CANDY CANES INSTEAD OF CRÈME DE MENTHE, MAKING IT PINK.

'SWIMMING POOL'- A SMALL BODY OF WATER COMPLETELY SURROUNDED BY NEIGHBOURS.

1¼ CUPS CHOCOLATE WAFER CRUMBS
¼ CUP SUGAR
⅓ CUP BUTTER

MIX ALL INGREDIENTS AND PRESS INTO BOTTOM AND SIDES OF 9 INCH PIE PLATE. BAKE IN OVEN AT 400° FOR 5 MINUTES.

1 ENVELOPE UNFLAVORED GELATIN
½ CUP SUGAR
DASH OF SALT
½ CUP COLD WATER
3 EGGS, SEPARATED
¼ CUP CRÈME DE MENTHE
¼ CUP CRÈME DE CACAO
1 CUP WHIPPING CREAM

IN DOUBLE BOILER MIX GELATIN, ¼ CUP SUGAR AND SALT. ADD WATER AND EGG YOLKS. STIR WELL UNTIL GELATIN IS DISSOLVED AND MIXTURE THICKENS SLIGHTLY. REMOVE FROM HEAT. STIR IN LIQUEURS. CHILL, STIRRING OCCASIONALLY UNTIL MIXTURE THICKENS SLIGHTLY. BEAT EGG WHITES STIFF. GRADUALLY ADD REMAINING SUGAR, BEAT UNTIL VERY STIFF. FOLD IN GELATIN MIXTURE. FOLD IN WHIPPED CREAM. TURN INTO SHELL. CHILL TWO HOURS IN FREEZER OR OVER NIGHT IN REFRIGERATOR.

CHOCOLATE MOCHA TORTE

- ⅞ CUP SUGAR
- 6 EGGS, SEPARATED
- ½ CUP FINE WAFER CRUMBS (VANILLA OR GRAHAM)
- ¼ CUP GRATED CHOCOLATE
- ¾ CUP CHOPPED WALNUTS
- 2 TBSPS. BRANDY OR RUM
- ½ TSP. DOUBLE ACTING BAKING POWDER
- ½ TSP. CINNAMON
- ¼ TSP. CLOVES
- ¼ TSP. NUTMEG

BEAT YOLKS, GRADUALLY ADDING SUGAR, THEN THE REMAINING DRY INGREDIENTS. WHIP WHITES UNTIL FLUFFY AND STIFF. FOLD INTO YOLK MIXTURE. BAKE IN 9" PAN WITH REMOVABLE SIDES FOR 1 HOUR AT 325°

FOR ICING SEE NEXT PAGE!

"DARLING, WHAT ARE YOU DOING, STANDING SO STILL?" "SHH! I'M TRYING OUT A NEW RECIPE. THE BOOK SAYS I MUSTN'T STIR FOR FIFTEEN MINUTES."

Chocolate Mocha Torte
ICING

16 LARGE MARSHMALLOWS
4 TBSPS. INSTANT COFFEE
1/3 CUP WATER
1/2 PINT WHIPPING CREAM, WHIPPED

MELT MARSHMALLOWS, COFFEE AND
WATER, STIRRING CONSTANTLY, THEN COOL.
FOLD WHIPPED CREAM INTO COOLED
MARSHMALLOW MIXTURE. CUT TORTE INTO
TWO LAYERS, FILLING TORTE. SAVE ENOUGH
TO ICE THE REST OF THE TORTE.
SPRINKLE WITH GRATED CHOCOLATE,
AND ADDITIONAL CHOPPED WALNUTS.

NEWLYWED COOKING TURKEY SUPPER
HEARS A KNOCK ON THE OVEN DOOR. SHE
OPENS THE DOOR, AND THE TURKEY SAYS;
"LOOK, LADY, EITHER TURN ON THE OVEN OR
GIVE ME BACK MY FEATHERS. IT'S COLD
IN HERE!"

CHERRIES JUBILEE

1 LB. DARK RED CHERRIES, OR 1 LARGE CAN DRAINED

1 TBSP. GRATED LEMON RIND

¼ CUP WHITE SUGAR

⅛ TSP. CINNAMON

¼ CUP OF KIRSCH OR CURAÇAO

1 TBSP. CORNSTARCH

3 TBSP. SUGAR

½ CUP BRANDY

VANILLA ICE CREAM

MARINATE CHERRIES WITH FIRST FOUR INGREDIENTS FOR 24 HOURS.

IN CHAFING DISH BLEND CORNSTARCH WITH CHERRIES, STIRRING UNTIL IT THICKENS. SPRINKLE WITH SUGAR AND ADD BRANDY. FLAME AND SERVE AT ONCE OVER ICE CREAM. FLAME AT THE TABLE TO ADD A SPECIAL TOUCH.

YOU'RE MIDDLE-AGED IF YOU CAN REMEMBER WHEN RADIOS PLUGGED IN, AND TOOTHBRUSHES DIDN'T.

Butter Brickle Dessert

- 2 cups flour
- ½ cup oatmeal
- ½ cup brown sugar
- 2 sticks of margarine
- 1 cup chopped pecans
- 1 jar Kraft caramel sauce
- 1 pint vanilla ice cream

Melt margarine. Add flour, oatmeal, brown sugar and pecans. Pat thin on a large cookie sheet and bake at 400° for 15 minutes. Crumble while hot and spread half on bottom of 9"x13" pan. Drizzle ½ jar of caramel topping over crumbs. Spread the ice cream over top, then put the remaining crumbs on ice cream and drizzle rest of caramel sauce on top. Freeze.

When your daughter marries, don't think of it as losing a daughter; think of it as gaining a bathroom!

A LIGHT AND DELICIOUS DESSERT. A FAVORITE OF MY FAMILY'S FOR AT LEAST THREE GENERATIONS (PROBABLY WHY IT'S CALLED <u>ICE BOX</u> PUDDING)

- 3/4 CUP GRAHAM WAFER CRUMBS
- 1 CUP (1/2 PT.) WHIPPING CREAM
- 3 EGGS
- 1 CUP SUGAR
- 1 LEMON
- 1 ORANGE
- 1 PKG. GELATIN

LINE A SMALL LOAF PAN WITH 1/2 CUP GRAHAM WAFER CRUMBS. IN A SMALL BOWL, ADD GELATIN TO JUICE OF LEMON AND ORANGE. SET IN A SLIGHTLY LARGER BOWL OF HOT WATER - HOT ENOUGH TO KEEP THE GELATIN MIXTURE LIQUID. CHECK THE HOT WATER FREQUENTLY. WHIP CREAM UNTIL STIFF. BEAT EGG WHITES UNTIL STIFF. GRADUALLY, ADD 1/2 CUP SUGAR, CONTINUE TO BEAT. BEAT EGG YOLKS IN A LARGE BOWL WITH 1/2 CUP SUGAR UNTIL LEMON COLOURED. ADD LEMON & ORANGE MIXTURE TO YOLKS. FOLD IN EGG WHITES. FOLD IN WHIPPED CREAM. POUR INTO LOAF PAN AND SPRINKLE WITH REMAINING GRAHAM WAFER CRUMBS. FREEZE FOR 1/2 DAY (AT LEAST) BEFORE SERVING. CONT'D NEXT PAGE....

ICE BOX PUDDING
CONTINUED

TO SERVE ICE BOX PUDDING:
REMOVE FROM PAN (LOOSEN EDGES AND
INVERT OVER SERVING PLATE) AND LEAVE
IN REFRIGERATOR AT LEAST ONE HOUR.
DECORATE WITH RED AND GREEN
MARASCHINO CHERRIES.

"YOU GAVE AWAY MY SECRET." "I DID NOT,
I EXCHANGED IT FOR ANOTHER."

RUM CREAM PIE

USE 2-8 INCH PIE SHELLS (PASTRY,
   GRAHAM WAFER OR CHOCOLATE WAFER)
   6   EGG YOLKS
   1   CUP SUGAR
   1   TBSP. GELATIN
   ½   CUP COLD WATER
   1   PINT CREAM, WHIPPED
   ½   CUP RUM

BEAT THE EGG YOLKS WITH THE SUGAR
UNTIL LIGHT AND FLUFFY. IN A SAUCEPAN
SOAK GELATIN IN WATER AND BRING TO A
BOIL. ADD TO THE EGG MIXTURE AND COOL.
ADD RUM TO WHIPPED CREAM AND FOLD INTO
EGG MIXTURE. POUR INTO COOLED PIE SHELLS.
SPRINKLE WITH SHREDDED CHOCOLATE. SERVE
AFTER CHILLING FOR SEVERAL HOURS.

FRESH STRAWBERRY PUFF PANCAKE

- ¼ CUP BUTTER OR MARGARINE
- 3 EGGS
- 1½ CUPS MILK
- ½ CUP SUGAR
- ¾ CUP FLOUR
- ¼ TSP. SALT
- 1 SMALL BASKET FRESH STRAWBERRIES

PLACE BUTTER IN 9" OVENPROOF FRYING PAN, CAKE PAN OR PIE PLATE. PUT PAN IN 425° OVEN UNTIL BUTTER MELTS AND BUBBLES (ABOUT 10 MINUTES). MEANWHILE, BEAT TOGETHER THE EGGS, MILK, 6 TBSP. SUGAR, FLOUR AND SALT UNTIL SMOOTH.

REMOVE PAN FROM OVEN AND IMMEDIATELY POUR MIXTURE INTO THE HOT PAN. RETURN TO OVEN AND BAKE AT 425° FOR 30 MINUTES OR UNTIL EGGS ARE PUFFED AND BROWNED.

SPRINKLE BERRIES WITH REMAINING SUGAR AND SPOON INTO CENTRE OF THE PANCAKE, WHEN DONE. SERVE IMMEDIATELY, CUT INTO WEDGES.

THE STORK IS TOO OFTEN HELD RESPONSIBLE FOR CIRCUMSTANCES THAT MIGHT BETTER BE ATTRIBUTED TO A LARK.

LIME PARFAIT PIE

CHOCOLATE WAFER CRUST (P. 207)
2   3 OZ. PKG. OF LIME JELLO
2   CUPS BOILING WATER
2   TBSPS. SHREDDED LIME PEEL
1/3 CUP LIME JUICE
1   QUART VANILLA ICE CREAM

DISSOLVE JELLO IN BOILING WATER. STIR
IN LIME PEEL AND JUICE. ADD ICE CREAM TO
JELLO IN A BLENDER OR LARGE BOWL WITH
A MIXMASTER AT HIGH SPEED, WHIPPING
UNTIL MELTED. CHILL UNTIL MIXTURE
BEGINS TO SET, THEN PILE INTO SHELL.
CHILL UNTIL FIRM. TOP WITH WHIPPED
CREAM AND COCONUT TO SERVE.

QUICK FROZEN DESSERT

3   TBSPS. BUTTER, MELTED
1½ CUPS GRAHAM WAFER CRUMBS
1   PINT VANILLA ICE CREAM.
1   TSP. CINNAMON.

COMBINE MELTED BUTTER AND CRUMBS
AND PAT INTO BOTTOM OF CAKE PAN.
BEAT VANILLA ICE CREAM AND ADD CINNAMON.
SPREAD OVER CRUST, SPRINKLE WITH ADDITIONAL
CRUMBS AND FREEZE UNTIL FIRM.

STRAWBERRY LEMON ANGEL TARTS

- 4   EGG WHITES
- 1/4   TSP. CREAM OF TARTAR
- 1   CUP SUGAR

BEAT EGG WHITES AND CREAM OF TARTAR UNTIL STIFF. ADD SUGAR _VERY_ GRADUALLY, BEATING THOROUGHLY AFTER EACH ADDITION, APPROXIMATELY 20 MINUTES IN ALL. GREASE COOKIE SHEETS WITH SHORTENING OR 'PAM' AND SPOON MERINGUE TO FORM 3" SHELLS, BUILDING UP SIDES WITH BACK OF SPOON. BAKE 20 MINUTES AT 250°, THEN AT 300° FOR 40 MINUTES. TURN OFF HEAT, OPEN OVEN DOOR AND LET SHELLS STAND FOR AT LEAST 40 MINUTES. IF MAKING AHEAD, STORE IN CARDBOARD SHIRTBOX IN COOL DRY PLACE.

SEE NEXT PAGE FOR FILLING.

HINT FOR ABOVE RECIPE:
WHEN BEATING EGG WHITES, ALWAYS WHIP THEM IN A GLASS BOWL OR IN A POT THAT HAS BEEN CLEANED IN SUDSY WATER TO REMOVE _ALL_ TRACES OF GREASE.
NEVER BEAT EGG WHITES IN PLASTIC BOWLS.

From Top To Bottom
Strawberry Lemon Tarts-Page 174
Lemon Berry Cake - Page 182
Angel Food Flan - Page 154

STRAWBERRY LEMON ANGEL TARTS

FILLING:

- 4 EGG YOLKS
- 1/3 CUP SUGAR
- 1/4 TSP. SALT
- 3 TBSPS. LEMON JUICE
- 1 TBSP. LEMON PEEL
- 1/2 PINT WHIPPING CREAM OR
  1 PKG. WHIPPED TOPPING
- FRESH STRAWBERRIES

COMBINE ALL INGREDIENTS EXCEPT WHIPPED CREAM AND STRAWBERRIES IN TOP OF DOUBLE BOILER. BRING TO BOIL AND SIMMER 2 MINUTES. COOL COMPLETELY. ADD WHIPPED CREAM. THIS MAY BE STORED FOR SEVERAL DAYS.

TO SERVE, SPOON FILLING IN EACH SHELL AND CHILL UP TO 8 HOURS. GARNISH WITH FRESH STRAWBERRIES AND EXTRA WHIPPED CREAM, IF DESIRED.

THIS IS A DELIGHTFULLY COOL DESSERT AND CAN BE MADE SEVERAL DAYS AHEAD.
(SEE PICTURE PAGE 176

A MAN USUALLY FEELS BETTER AFTER A FEW WINKS, ESPECIALLY IF SHE WINKS BACK.

STRAWBERRY CRÈPES

1 EGG
1¼ CUPS MILK
1 TBSP. MELTED BUTTER
1¼ CUPS SIFTED FLOUR
½ TSP. SALT
4 CUPS STRAWBERRIES
3 FIRM, RIPE BANANAS
¾ CUP WATER
2 TBSPS. CORNSTARCH
½ CUP SUGAR
⅓ CUP CURACAO

CRÈPES:

BEAT EGG, MILK, BUTTER, FLOUR AND SALT UNTIL SMOOTH. LIGHTLY GREASE CRÈPE PAN OR SMALL SKILLET WITH OIL OR 'PAM. HEAT SKILLET - REMOVE FROM HEAT AND POUR IN ¼ CUP OF BATTER, TILTING PAN TO COVER BOTTOM QUICKLY. RETURN TO HEAT, BROWNING ON ONE SIDE ONLY, AND COOL ON PAPER TOWEL. MAKE 7 MORE CRÈPES. STACK BETWEEN WAX PAPER. CRÈPES MAY BE FROZEN.

FOR STRAWBERRY GLAZE SEE NEXT PAGE

ONLY ONE PERFECT WOMAN EVER EXISTED - THE WOMAN YOUR HUSBAND COULD HAVE MARRIED.

STRAWBERRY CRÈPE GLAZE

CRUSH 2 CUPS OF STRAWBERRIES IN SAUCEPAN, ADD WATER AND BRING TO A BOIL. SIMMER FOR 2 MINUTES. SIEVE. IN SAME SAUCEPAN, COMBINE SUGAR AND CORN STARCH. ADD SIEVED BERRIES, STIRRING CONSTANTLY, UNTIL MIXTURE BUBBLES. REMOVE FROM HEAT AND ADD CURAÇAO.

RESERVE 1 CUP OF GLAZE. STIR 1 CUP SLICED BERRIES INTO REMAINING GLAZE AND SPREAD 3 TBSPS. ON UNBROWNED SIDE OF EACH CRÈPE, PLACING THEM IN CHAFING OR SERVING DISH. ADD LAST CUP OF HALVED STRAWBERRIES AND SLICED BANANAS, POURING REMAINING GLAZE OVER ALL. COVER AND KEEP WARM TILL SERVING TIME. SERVES 8.

THE HEIGHT OF MISERY IS GOING UP TO THE ATTIC, READING YOUR HUSBAND'S OLD LOVE LETTERS AND FINDING THEY'RE DATED LAST WEEK.

Chocolate Torte Royale

MERINGUE

2 EGG WHITES
½ TSP. VINEGAR
SALT
½ CUP SUGAR
½ TSP. CINNAMON

ADD SALT AND CINNAMON TO EGG WHITES AND BEAT UNTIL PEAKS FORM. GRADUALLY ADD SUGAR AND VINEGAR, BEATING WELL AFTER EACH ADDITION, UNTIL MERINGUE IS STIFF. SPREAD ON BROWN PAPER IN AN 8" CIRCLE AND BAKE AT 275° FOR 1 HOUR. TURN OVEN OFF, LET COOL IN OVEN FOR 2 HOURS.

NOTE! THIS RECIPE IS CONTINUED NEXT PAGE.

YOUNG BOY EXPLAINING HOW SIMPLE IT IS TO MAKE BREAD; "YOU JUST ADD THE YEAST TO THE FLOUR, PUNCH IT AROUND, PUT IT IN A BOWL AND LET IT GO TO THE WEST!"

FILLING

6 OZ. SEMI-SWEET CHOCOLATE
2 EGG YOLKS
1/4 CUP WATER
1 CUP HEAVY CREAM
1/4 CUP SUGAR
1/4 TSP. CINNAMON
CHOPPED PECANS

MELT CHOCOLATE WITH WATER. SPREAD 2 TBSPS. OVER BOTTOM OF SHELL. TO REMAINING CHOCOLATE ADD BEATEN YOLKS, BLEND WELL AND CHILL UNTIL THICK. WHIP CREAM, SUGAR AND CINNAMON. FOLD INTO CHOCOLATE MIXTURE. SPREAD INTO SHELL AND CHILL. GARNISH WITH WHIPPED CREAM AND CHOPPED PECANS.

THE ONLY WAY TO GET OUT OF BED EVERY MORNING WITH A SMILE ON YOUR FACE IS TO GO TO BED AT NIGHT WITH A COAT HANGER IN YOUR MOUTH.

LEMONBERRY CAKE

18 OZ. UNSWEETENED FROZEN
      BLUEBERRIES, THAWED
1 PKG. 2 LAYER LEMON CAKE MIX
8 OZ. LEMON OR VANILLA YOGURT
4 EGGS

GLAZE:

1 CUP ICING SUGAR
4 TSP. MILK

BLUEBERRY SAUCE:

1 CUP SUGAR
2 TBSPS. CORNSTARCH
1 CUP WATER
3 TBSPS. LEMON JUICE
  WHIPPED CREAM

RINSE AND DRAIN BERRIES, RESERVING
LIQUID. COMBINE CAKE MIX, EGGS AND YOGURT,
BEATING 2 MINUTES. FOLD IN HALF OF DRAINED
BERRIES. BAKE IN GREASED 10" TUBE OR BUNDT
PAN AT 350° FOR 45 MINUTES, OR UNTIL DONE.
DO NOT INVERT PAN, OR REMOVE, UNTIL CAKE IS
COOL. MAKE GLAZE AND DRIZZLE OVER CAKE.
CONTINUED NEXT PAGE!

THE HONEYMOON IS OVER WHEN THE DOG
BRINGS HIM HIS SLIPPERS AND THE WIFE
BARKS AT HIM.

LEMONBERRY CAKE

CONTINUED!

IN PAN, COMBINE SUGAR, CORNSTARCH, THEN THE WATER. BRING TO BOIL AND COOK TWO MINUTES. ADD BLUEBERRIES AND JUICE. ADDITIONAL CORNSTARCH MAY BE ADDED IF A THICKER SAUCE IS DESIRED.

TO SERVE, REHEAT SAUCE AND POUR OVER CAKE SLICES ON SERVING PLATES, AND ADD A DAB OF WHIPPED CREAM TO EACH SERVING. SEE PICTURE PAGE 176.

BRANDIED PEACHES

1	28 OZ. TIN OF PEACH HALVES
2	TBSPS. SYRUP FROM PEACHES
4	TBSPS. BUTTER
½	CUP BROWN SUGAR
¼	TSP. CINNAMON
¼	CUP BRANDY

DRAIN PEACHES, RESERVING 2 TBSPS. OF SYRUP. PLACE IN SHALLOW BAKING DISH. COMBINE ALL INGREDIENTS AND SPOON OVER PEACHES. BAKE AT 350° FOR 25 TO 30 MINUTES, BASTING OCCASIONALLY.

SERVE OVER VANILLA ICE CREAM, OR WITH HEAPING TEASPOON OF SOUR CREAM IN EACH CENTRE, GARNISHED WITH NUTMEG.

BLUEBERRY DELIGHT

YOU MAY ALSO USE STRAWBERRY OR RASPBERRY PIE FILLING. THIS IS A LIGHT, REFRESHING DESSERT. SERVES 12

- 2½ CUPS GRAHAM WAFER CRUMBS
- ½ CUP BUTTER
- 1 TBSP. SUGAR
- BLUEBERRY PIE FILLING
- ½ PINT WHIPPING CREAM, WHIPPED
- 1½ CUPS ICING SUGAR

BLEND FIRST THREE INGREDIENTS TOGETHER AND PUT IN 9" x 13" PAN. BAKE AT 350° FOR 10 MINUTES. BLEND WHIPPED CREAM AND ICING SUGAR TOGETHER AND POUR MIXTURE ON COOLED WAFER CRUST. POUR CANNED BLUEBERRY FILLING ON TOP AND CHILL UNTIL READY TO SERVE. MAY BE SERVED WITH A SMALL DAB OF WHIPPED CREAM ON TOP.

CHAOS IS SIX WOMEN PLUS ONE LUNCHEON CHECK.

PEPPERMINT ICE CREAM PIE

1   PKG. (6 OZ.) SEMI-SWEET
         CHOCOLATE CHIPS
2   TBSPS. BUTTER, SOFTENED
2   TBSPS. POWDERED SUGAR
1   QUART PEPPERMINT
         ICE CREAM, SOFTENED
    CHOCOLATE SHAVINGS FOR TOPPING.

LINE A 9 INCH PIE PAN BY PRESSING A
12 INCH SQUARE OF HEAVY ALUMINUM FOIL
ON BOTTOM, SIDES AND OVER RIM. SPRINKLE
CHIPS EVENLY ON FOIL LINER. PUT IN 250°
OVEN FOR 5 MINUTES, ABSOLUTELY NO
LONGER. BLEND BUTTER INTO MELTED
CHOCOLATE. ADD POWDERED SUGAR; BLEND
AGAIN UNTIL MIXTURE THICKENS SLIGHTLY.
SPREAD MIXTURE THINLY OVER BOTTOM
AND UP SIDES OF FOIL LINER. REFRIGERATE
30 MINUTES FOR CHOCOLATE SHELL TO
HARDEN. PEEL FOIL FROM SHELL AND
RETURN SHELL TO PIE PAN. FILL WITH ICE
CREAM; DECORATE WITH SHAVED CHOCOLATE.
STORE IN FREEZER UNTIL READY TO
SERVE.   SERVES 6 TO 8

PEPPERMINT BAR

BASE:

½ CUP BUTTER
2 EGGS
1 CUP WHITE SUGAR
1 TSP. SALT
½ TSP. PEPPERMINT EXTRACT
2 SQUARES UNSWEETENED CHOCOLATE
½ CUP FLOUR

MELT BUTTER AND CHOCOLATE. REMOVE FROM HEAT AND ADD BEATEN EGGS AND BEAT WELL. ADD SUGAR, PEPPERMINT, FLOUR AND SALT. BEAT WELL. POUR INTO GREASED 9" x 9" PAN. BAKE AT 350° FOR 20 MINUTES. COOL.

2ND LAYER:

1 CUP ICING SUGAR
2 HEAPING TBSPS. BUTTER
1 TBSP. MILK OR CREAM
1 TBSP. PEPPERMINT EXTRACT
FEW DROPS GREEN FOOD COLOURING,
    IF DESIRED

MIX SUGAR AND BUTTER UNTIL SMOOTH. ADD REMAINING INGREDIENTS AND MIX WELL. SPREAD ON FIRST LAYER (BASE) AND COOL UNTIL SET. (CONTINUED NEXT PAGE!)

PEPPERMINT BAR

CONTINUED!

TOP LAYER:

2   SQUARES SEMI-SWEET CHOCOLATE
2   TBSPS. BUTTER

MELT TOGETHER. COOL AND DRIZZLE OVER SECOND LAYER.

STRAWBERRY ANGEL FOOD CAKE

1   ANGEL FOOD MIX
1   PKG. STRAWBERRY JELLO
    (RASPBERRY MAY BE USED)
1   PKG. FROZEN STRAWBERRIES
½   PINT WHIPPING CREAM
1   CUP WATER (BOILING)

MAKE ANGEL FOOD CAKE. DISSOLVE JELLO IN BOILING WATER. ADD SEMI-THAWED BERRIES. MIX WELL. PUT IN REFRIGERATOR WHEN THIS BEGINS TO SET BLEND IN WHIPPED CREAM. TEAR CAKE INTO BITE-SIZED PIECES AND ARRANGE IN ANGEL FOOD PAN. POUR BERRY MIXTURE AROUND SO THAT MIXTURE COVERS IT ALL. SET IN REFRIGERATOR FOR 24 HOURS. UNMOLD AND SERVE. ADD ADDITIONAL BERRIES AND WHIPPED CREAM.
THIS IS A LIGHT AND REFRESHING DESSERT.

PEPPERMINT CANDY DESSERT

THIS DESSERT IS VERY RICH—SO GO EASY ON THE SIZE OF THE SERVING.

- 2 CUPS VANILLA WAFER CRUMBS
- 1/4 CUP MELTED BUTTER
- 1/2 CUP BUTTER
- 1 1/2 CUPS ICING SUGAR
- 3 EGGS, SLIGHTLY BEATEN
- 3 SQUARES UNSWEETENED CHOCOLATE, MELTED
- 1 1/2 CUPS WHIPPING CREAM, WHIPPED
- 1 PKG. MINIATURE MARSHMALLOWS
- 1 CRUSHED PEPPERMINT CANDY STICK.

MAKE A CRUST OF WAFER CRUMBS AND MELTED BUTTER. PAT INTO 9" x 13" PAN AND REFRIGERATE. CREAM TOGETHER SUGAR, 1/2 CUP BUTTER, THEN ADD EGGS AND CHOCOLATE. BEAT WELL THEN SPOON OVER CRUST, REFRIGERATE. COMBINE WHIPPED CREAM AND MARSHMALLOWS, AND SPOON OVER CHOCOLATE LAYER. WHEN SERVING, SPRINKLE CRUSHED PEPPERMINT CANDY STICK OVER TOP.

Marshmallow Coffee Dessert

Vanilla Wafers
½ LB. Marshmallows
½ Cup of Strong Coffee
½ Pint of Whipping Cream,
    Whipped.

Cut marshmallows with scissors in 4 pieces and pour hot coffee over them. When cool, add whipped cream. Line pie plate with vanilla wafers and pour in mixture. Sprinkle rolled wafers on top. Refrigerate till serving time. Serves 8.

If owls are so smart, how come they don't get off the night shift?

Lemon Butter

For cake fillings and tarts.
5 Eggs, well beaten
½ LB. Butter
1 Cup Sugar
4 Lemons

Melt butter and sugar. Grate lemon rind, squeeze juice. Add to butter mixture, then pour in eggs, beating well over medium heat until thick.

Deluxe Sauce
(for Angel Cakes)

- ½ cup butter
- ½ cup flour
- ½ cup sugar
- pinch of salt
- 1 cup milk
- 2 egg yolks
- 2 egg whites
- 2 tbsps. sugar
- rind of 1 orange
- 1 cup whipping cream, whipped
- 1 tsp. vanilla or orange juice
- 1 prepared angel food cake

Melt butter in double boiler, stirring in flour and ½ cup sugar and salt. Add milk, and cook for 10 minutes. Remove from heat and beat in egg yolks. Allow to cool completely. Beat in stiffly beaten egg whites and 2 tbsps. sugar. Add whipped cream, orange peel and flavoring. Spoon over cake. Refrigerate until serving time.

Where do bad little girls go? Bad little girls go almost everywhere they want to.

CREAMY VANILLA FROSTING

- 2 TBSPS. SHORTENING
- ½ TSP. SALT
- 1 TSP. VANILLA
- 1½ CUPS ICING SUGAR
- 2 TBSPS. MILK
- CINNAMON TO TASTE

MIX SHORTENING, SALT, VANILLA AND ½ CUP SUGAR. ADD MILK AND THE REST OF THE SUGAR.

'SUNBURN' - GETTING WHAT YOU BASKED FOR.

ISLA'S ICING

THIS ICING NEVER GETS HARD. IT'S REALLY GREAT ON SPICE CAKE.

- 4 TBSPS. SOFT BUTTER
- 6 TBSPS. ICING SUGAR
- 2 TSPS. MILK (I SAID TEASPOONS)
- 2 TSPS. WATER

BEAT IN MIXMASTER AT HIGH SPEED FOR 5 MINUTES. UNTIL FLUFFY. ENOUGH FOR 9" SQUARE CAKE.

Chocolate Fudge

1 Package Chocolate Chips
2 Cups White Sugar
2/3 Cup Evaporated Milk
12 Marshmallows-Regular Size
1/2 Cup Butter
Dash of Salt
1 Tsp. Vanilla

Cook all ingredients except chocolate chips and vanilla, stirring over medium heat until mixture comes to a boil. Boil for 5 minutes. Remove from heat — add chocolate chips and vanilla. Pour into a 8"x8" pan. Cool and cut into squares. This is a super treat for your sweet tooth.

Fudge Scotch Squares

1½ Cups Graham Cracker Crumbs
1 14 oz. Can Borden Eagle Brand- Condensed Sweetened Milk
1 Cup Semi-Sweet Chocolate Chips
1 Cup Butterscotch Chips
1 Cup Coarsely Chopped Walnuts

Mix well and pat mixture into a well greased 9 inch pan. Bake at 350° for 30 to 35 minutes. Cool before serving.

RASPBERRY SQUARES

1 CUP FLOUR
1 TBSP. MILK
1 EGG
½ TSP. SALT
1 TSP. BAKING POWDER
½ CUP BUTTER
STRAWBERRY OR RASPBERRY JAM

MIX INGREDIENTS LIKE A PIE DOUGH AND ROLL TO PAN SIZE. 9"x13". SPREAD A THIN LAYER OF JAM ON TOP.

1 CUP WHITE SUGAR
¼ CUP BUTTER, MELTED
1 TSP. VANILLA
1½ CUPS COCONUT
1 BEATEN EGG

MIX INGREDIENTS WELL AND SPREAD OVER JAM. BAKE IN 350° OVEN FOR 25 MINUTES. CUT INTO SQUARES WHEN WARM.

YOU CAN TELL MALE PANCAKES FROM FEMALE PANCAKES BY NOTICING WHICH ONES ARE STACKED.

THIS SQUARE IS ALWAYS A HIT — TRY IT WITH YOUR CHRISTMAS BAKING.

CRUST:

- 1⅓ CUPS FLOUR
- 1 TBSP. SUGAR (WHITE)
- ¾ CUP BUTTER

COMBINE FLOUR AND SUGAR. CUT IN BUTTER (MEALY TEXTURED.) PRESS FIRMLY INTO BOTTOM OF LIGHTLY GREASED PAN. BAKE AT 350° FOR 20 MINUTES.

FILLING:

- 2 EGGS
- 1 CUP BROWN SUGAR
- 1 TSP. VANILLA
- 1 CUP SHREDDED COCONUT
- ⅔ CUP WALNUTS, CHOPPED
- ¼ CUP GLACE CHERRIES, SNIPPED
- 3 TBSPS. FLOUR
- 1 TSP. BAKING POWDER
- PINCH OF SALT

BEAT EGGS, GRADUALLY ADDING SUGAR AND VANILLA. SIFT FLOUR, BAKING POWDER AND SALT AND ADD TO SUGAR MIXTURE. ADD REMAINING INGREDIENTS. SPREAD OVER CRUST AND RETURN TO OVEN (LOWER TO 300°). BAKE 25 TO 30 MINUTES UNTIL TOP IS SET AND LIGHTLY BROWN.

FOR ICING SEE NEXT PAGE!

DREAM SLICE

CONTINUED!

BUTTER ICING:

¼ CUP BUTTER
2½ CUPS ICING SUGAR
3 TBSPS. CREAM

CREAM BUTTER. ADD ICING SUGAR. ALTERNATELY WITH CREAM UNTIL SPREADING CONSISTENCY IS REACHED. SPREAD OVER COOLED CAKE. SEE PICTURE PAGE 141.

SOME NIGHTS THE ONLY GOOD THINGS ON T.V. ARE THE VASE AND THE CLOCK!

CHEESE SQUARES

¼ LB. BUTTER
¼ LB. VELVEETA CHEESE
¼ CUP BROWN SUGAR
1¾ CUPS FLOUR
1½ TSP. BAKING POWDER
½ TSP. SALT
JELLY (CRABAPPLE, APPLE OR RASPBERRY)

COMBINE INGREDIENTS. PAT ¾ OF MIXTURE IN AN 8" x 8" PAN. COVER WITH JAM OR JELLY. CRUMBLE REST OF MIXTURE ON TOP. BAKE 25 MINUTES AT 300°.

MAGIC Cookie Bars

Don't make these if you can't avoid temptation - they're too yummy.

- 2 cups crushed corn flakes
- 3 tbsps. sugar
- ½ cup butter

Mix ingredients thoroughly and pat into a 9" x 9" pan.

- 1 cup chocolate chips
- 1½ cups coconut
- 1 cup chopped pecans
- 1 14oz. can Eagle Brand, condensed milk.

Sprinkle above ingredients over first mixture in order, then drizzle condensed milk over all. Bake at 350° for 30 to 35 minutes. See picture page 141.

PEANUT BUTTER SLICE

A real hit with children.

- ½ cup butter
- 1 cup peanut butter
- 2 pkg. butterscotch chips
- 2 cups miniature marshmallows

Melt butter, peanut butter and chips in top of double boiler. Cool and add marshmallows. Put in 8" x 8" pan. Refrigerate.

PEANUT BUTTER CRUNCHIES

1 CUP PEANUT BUTTER
½ CUP CORN SYRUP
½ CUP BROWN SUGAR
1 TSP. SALT
2 CUPS CORN FLAKES
1 CUP RICE KRISPIES

PLACE SUGAR AND SYRUP IN DOUBLE BOILER, MELT. ADD PEANUT BUTTER, CORN FLAKES AND KRISPIES. PAT IN 8"×8" GREASED PAN AND REFRIGERATE.

MEXICAN WEDDING CAKE

1 CUP SOFT BUTTER
½ CUP SUGAR
½ TSP. SALT
2 CUPS SIFTED FLOUR
1½ CUPS GROUND ALMONDS
    (24 OZ. PKG. OR 226 GRAMS)
2 TSPS. VANILLA

MIX WELL AND REFRIGERATE FOR 1 HOUR. ROLL INTO SMALL BALLS. BAKE AT 325° FOR 15 MINUTES. ROLL IN ICING SUGAR WHILE HOT.

1ST LAYER:

- ½ CUP BUTTER
- ¼ CUP BROWN SUGAR
- 3 TBSPS. COCOA
- 1 BEATEN EGG
- 2 CUPS GRAHAM WAFER CRUMBS
- 1 CUP COCONUT
- ½ CUP CHOPPED WALNUTS

COMBINE, PUT IN 9" SQUARE PAN AND CHILL FOR ½ HOUR.

2ND LAYER:

- 2 CUPS ICING SUGAR
- ¼ CUP BUTTER
- ¼ CUP CREAM OR MILK
- 2 TBSPS. BIRD'S CUSTARD POWDER

COMBINE ALL INGREDIENTS, BEATING UNTIL SMOOTH AND FLUFFY, THEN SPREAD CAREFULLY ON TOP OF FIRST LAYER.

3RD LAYER:

- 3 CHOCOLATE SQUARES (SWEET OR SEMI-SWEET)
- ¼ CUP BUTTER, MELTED

MELT CHOCOLATE AND BUTTER TOGETHER, THEN SPREAD OVER SECOND LAYER AND CHILL.

AS THIS IS A VERY RICH SQUARE, IT SHOULD BE CUT INTO SMALL 1" PIECES. (PICTURE PAGE 141)

SHORTBREAD TARTS
(SEE PICTURE PAGE 141)

USE TINY MUFFIN TINS - APPROXIMATELY
1½" DIAMETER. THIS WILL MAKE ABOUT 3 DOZ.

    1   CUP BUTTER
    ½   CUP ICING SUGAR
    1½ CUPS FLOUR
    1   TBSP. CORNSTARCH

MIX INGREDIENTS IN MIXMASTER. DON'T
ROLL BUT PAT INTO MUFFIN TINS WITH
YOUR FINGERS TO FORM SHELL. PRICK THE
BOTTOMS WITH A FORK AND BAKE 20 MINUTES
AT 300° TO 325°. DURING BAKING TIME,
PRICK BOTTOMS AGAIN IF THE SHELLS
PUFF UP. THESE MAY BE MADE IN LARGE
QUANTITY AND FROZEN. FILLINGS BELOW.

LEMON CHEESE FILLING

    2   EGGS
    2   TBSPS. BUTTER
    1   CUP SUGAR
    JUICE OF 2 LEMONS AND A BIT OF PEEL

COMBINE ALL INGREDIENTS IN PAN AND BRING
TO BOIL. REDUCE HEAT AND COOK, STIRRING
CONSTANTLY FOR 15 MINUTES. COVER AND COOL
IN REFRIGERATOR. THIS FILLING WILL KEEP
WELL IN REFRIGERATOR FOR A LONG TIME. ONLY
FILL THE SHELLS AS THEY ARE REQUIRED.

(CONTINUED NEXT PAGE)

SHORTBREAD TARTS

ALTERNATE FILLING!
RUM MINCEMEAT FILLING

1 BOTTLE OF PREPARED MINCEMEAT
¼ CUP RUM, OR TO TASTE

COMBINE MINCEMEAT AND RUM IN SAUCEPAN AND HEAT TILL WARM.

BUTTER TARTS

THESE ARE EXCEPTIONAL! FOR THESE USE FROZEN SHELLS OR YOUR OWN PASTRY RECIPE.

- 1 CUP WHITE SUGAR
- 1 CUP SEEDLESS RAISINS
- 2 EGGS
- 1 TSP. VANILLA
- ⅓ CUP BUTTER
- 4 TBSPS. CREAM OR HALF & HALF
- ½ CUP BROKEN WALNUTS

BEAT EGGS. COMBINE WITH REMAINING INGREDIENTS EXCEPT NUTS, AND BOIL AT MEDIUM HEAT FOR 3 MINUTES. ADD NUTS. FILL UNBAKED TART SHELLS AND BAKE FOR 15 MINUTES AT 375°

VERNA'S CHOCOLATE SQUARES

1 PKG. DAD'S COCONUT (OR PLAIN) COOKIES
¼ CUP BUTTER, MELTED
2 SQUARES SEMI-SWEET CHOCOLATE
¼ CUP MELTED BUTTER
1½ CUPS ICING SUGAR
1 TSP. VANILLA
1 EGG, BEATEN
1 CUP CHOPPED WALNUTS

CRUSH COOKIES, ADD MELTED ¼ CUP BUTTER AND PUT ⅔ INTO PAN. BAKE 5 MINUTES AT 300°. MIX CHOCOLATE SQUARES AND ¼ CUP MELTED BUTTER. ADD ICING SUGAR, VANILLA, EGG AND WALNUTS. SPREAD OVER FIRST LAYER AND SPRINKLE WITH REMAINING CRUMBS. REFRIGERATE.
PICTURE PAGE 141.

IF YOU THINK ENGLISH IS AN EASY LANGUAGE TO LEARN, THEN HOW COME "FAT CHANCE" MEANS THE SAME AS "SLIM CHANCE".

PREPARATION:

A THREE-SIZED CHRISTMAS CAKE TIN SET MUST BE LINED, BOTTOMS AND SIDES, WITH BUTTERED BROWN PAPER. CUT THE PAPER TO SIZE. THE NIGHT BEFORE YOU MAKE THIS CAKE, POUR BOILING WATER OVER THE RAISINS, DRAIN, AND DRY ON PAPER TOWELLING. LEAVE THESE OVERNIGHT. THE FRUIT IN THE RECIPE IS FLOURED WITH ½ THE AMOUNT OF FLOUR CALLED FOR IN THE RECIPE.

- ½ LB. BUTTER
- 1½ CUPS WHITE SUGAR
- 6 EGGS
- ½ CUP ORANGE JUICE
- 3 CUPS REGULAR FLOUR, SIFTED
- 1 TSP. BAKING POWDER
- 1 TSP. SALT
- JUICE AND RIND OF 1 LEMON
- ½ LB. RED GLACE CHERRIES
- ½ LB. GREEN GLACE CHERRIES
- ½ LB. CITRON PEEL
- 2 SLICES EACH, RED AND GREEN PINEAPPLE, CUT UP
- 2 LBS. BLANCHED SULTANA RAISINS
- ½ LB. BLANCHED ALMONDS

CONTINUED NEXT PAGE!

LIGHT CHRISTMAS CAKE

CONTINUED!

USE ½ OF THE FLOUR TO COVER CHERRIES, CITRON PEEL, PINEAPPLE, AND WELL-DRIED RAISINS. CREAM SUGAR AND BUTTER, ADD BEATEN EGGS, ORANGE AND LEMON JUICE, AND RIND. ADD REMAINING FLOUR. MIX WELL. ADD FLOURED FRUIT AND CHOPPED ALMONDS. BAKE AT 275° FOR TWO HOURS. TEST FOR DONENESS. STORE IN A COOL PLACE.

PRUNE CAKE

- 2 CUPS SELF-RISING FLOUR
- 2 CUPS SUGAR
- 1 TSP. CINNAMON
- 1 TSP. NUTMEG
- 1 TSP. ALLSPICE
- 1 CUP SALAD OIL
- 2 EGGS
- 8 OZ. CAN, PRUNES (PUREED BABY FOOD)
- 1 CUP CHOPPED PECANS

COMBINE ALL INGREDIENTS, BEATING AT MEDIUM SPEED UNTIL BLENDED. DO NOT OVER MIX. POUR INTO 10 INCH BUNDT PAN, WELL-GREASED AND LIGHTLY FLOURED. BAKE AT 350° FOR APPROXIMATELY 1 HOUR.

APPLESAUCE SPICE CAKE

2½ CUPS SIFTED FLOUR
2 CUPS SUGAR
1½ TSP. SALT
1½ TSP. BAKING SODA
¼ TSP. BAKING POWDER
1 TSP. CINNAMON
½ TSP. GROUND CLOVES
½ TSP. ALLSPICE
1½ CUPS APPLESAUCE
½ CUP SHORTENING
½ CUP WATER (SEE BELOW)
2 EGGS
1 CUP RAISINS
½ CUP CHOPPED WALNUTS OR PECANS

PUT RAISINS AND SPICES IN A POT. ADD WATER TO 2" ABOVE RAISINS. BOIL FOR 20 MINUTES. COOL, THEN DRAIN, RESERVING LIQUID. ADD WATER TO LIQUID, IF NEEDED, TO MAKE ½ CUP OF LIQUID. IN BOWL, MIX TOGETHER FIRST 5 INGREDIENTS. ADD APPLESAUCE, SHORTENING AND RESERVED LIQUID. ADD EGGS — BEAT 2 MINUTES. STIR IN RAISINS AND NUTS. BAKE IN 2 LOAF PANS OR LARGE CAKE PAN AT 350° FOR 50 TO 60 MINUTES. KEEPS VERY WELL.

BROWNIES

1 CUP WHITE SUGAR
PINCH OF SALT
5 TBSPS. BUTTER
2 EGGS, BEATEN
4 TBSPS. COCOA
2/3 CUP FLOUR
1/3 CUP WHIPPING CREAM
1 TSP. VANILLA
1/2 CUP CHOPPED WALNUTS

CREAM SUGAR AND BUTTER. ADD REMAINING INGREDIENTS AND MIX WELL. POUR INTO GREASED 8 INCH PAN. BAKE AT 350° FOR 20 TO 25 MINUTES.

ICING FOR BROWNIES

2 TBSPS. COCOA
2 TBSPS. BUTTER
3 TBSPS. COFFEE (LIQUID)
2 TSPS. VANILLA
ICING SUGAR

MIX ABOVE INGREDIENTS AND ADD ICING SUGAR UNTIL IT IS THE CONSISTENCY OF ICING

SUPER CHOCOLATE CAKE

THIS IS A TRULY DELICIOUS HOME-MADE CAKE.

1	CUP WHITE SUGAR
3	TBSPS. BUTTER
1	EGG
½	CUP COCOA-FILL WITH BOILING WATER TO MAKE ONE CUP OF LIQUID.
1	CUP FLOUR
1	TSP. BAKING POWDER
½	TSP. SODA
½	CUP BOILING WATER

CREAM SUGAR AND BUTTER; ADD BEATEN EGG AND COCOA LIQUID. MIX SODA AND BOILING WATER. ADD THIS AND REMAINING INGREDIENTS, MIX WELL, AND POUR INTO GREASED 9" x 9" PAN. BAKE FOR 30 MINUTES AT 350°

A BOY IS GROWN WHEN HE'D RATHER STEAL A KISS THAN SECOND BASE.

LAZY DAISY CAKE

2 EGGS
1 CUP SUGAR
1 TSP. VANILLA
1 CUP FLOUR
1 TSP. BAKING POWDER
¼ TSP. SALT
½ CUP MILK
1 TBSP. BUTTER

BEAT EGGS, SUGAR AND VANILLA UNTIL LEMON COLOURED. SIFT FLOUR, BAKING POWDER AND SALT, ADD TO EGG MIXTURE, MIXING BY HAND UNTIL COMBINED. HEAT (TO BOILING) THE MILK AND BUTTER. ADD ALL AT ONCE TO FIRST MIXTURE, BEATING ONLY UNTIL SMOOTH. BAKE AT 350° FOR 30 MINUTES, IN 8"×8" GREASED PAN.

TOPPING:

3 TBSPS. MELTED BUTTER
5 TBSPS. BROWN SUGAR
2 TBSPS. CREAM
½ CUP COCONUT

COMBINE ALL INGREDIENTS IN A PAN UNTIL MELTED. SPREAD ON TOP OF BAKED CAKE AND BROWN UNDER BROILER, WATCHING CAREFULLY THAT IT DOESN'T BURN.

SOCIAL APPLE BETTY

EVERYONE LOVES THIS OLD ENGLISH RECIPE. BE SURE TO SERVE IT WARM, WITH WHIPPING CREAM OR ICE CREAM.

6 TO 7 APPLES, PEELED AND SLICED
CINNAMON - TO TASTE

CRUST:
1/2 CUP BUTTER
SCANT CUP - BROWN SUGAR
3/4 CUP FLOUR

FILL SMALL CASSEROLE DISH (1 1/2 QUARTS) 2/3 FULL WITH SLICED APPLES ADDING THE CINNAMON TO TASTE. IF THE APPLES ARE TART, YOU MAY WANT TO ADD SOME WHITE SUGAR.

CRUST

CREAM BUTTER AND BROWN SUGAR. ADD FLOUR AND RUB TO A CRUMBLY MIXER. SPRINKLE MIXTURE OVER APPLES AND PAT FIRMLY INTO A CRUST. BAKE AT 350° FOR 40 MINUTES. SERVES SIX.

A HIGHBROW IS A PERSON WHO CAN LISTEN TO THE "WILLIAM TELL OVERTURE" WITHOUT THINKING OF THE LONE RANGER!

GRAHAM CRACKER CRUMB CRUST

1¼ CUPS GRAHAM CRUMBS
¼ CUP BROWN SUGAR
⅓ CUP MELTED BUTTER OR MARGARINE
½ TSP. CINNAMON (OPTIONAL)

MIX TOGETHER AND PRESS INTO 8 OR 9 INCH PIE PLATE. BAKE AT 300° FOR 5 TO 8 MINUTES. COOL.

STATISTICS PROVE THAT MORE AND MORE PEOPLE ARE MARRYING AT AN EARLY URGE.

CHOCOLATE WAFER CRUMB CRUST

1¼ CUPS CRUSHED CHRISTIE
CHOCOLATE WAFERS
(USE BLENDER OR ROLL WITH ROLLING PIN ON WAX PAPER)
⅓ CUP MELTED BUTTER OR MARGARINE.

MIX TOGETHER AND PRESS INTO 8 OR 9 INCH PIE PLATE. BAKE AT 300° FOR 5 TO 8 MINUTES. COOL.

PASTRY SHELLS

FOR ENTREES OR APPETIZERS

1	CUP COLD WATER
½	CUP BUTTER
4	EGGS (ROOM TEMPERATURE)
½	TSP. SALT
1	CUP SIFTED FLOUR

COMBINE WATER, BUTTER AND SALT IN A PAN. BRING TO A BOIL, STIRRING CONSTANTLY, AND ADD FLOUR. REMOVE FROM HEAT. STIR INTO A SMOOTH BALL. RETURN TO HEAT, AT MEDIUM TEMPERATURE, AND BEAT FOR 1 MINUTE. COOL APPROXIMATELY 5 MINUTES. BEAT IN EGGS ONE AT A TIME, STIRRING THOROUGHLY AFTER EACH ADDITION. COVER AND LET STAND IN COOL PLACE UNTIL COOL. PLACE ½ TSP. DOUGH FOR EACH SHELL AT INTERVALS ON GREASED COOKIE SHEET. BAKE AT 425° FOR ABOUT 30 MINUTES. WHEN BAKED, PRICK TOP OF EACH SHELL TO ALLOW AIR TO ESCAPE. LEAVE IN OVEN, HEAT TURNED OFF, FOR 10 MINUTES. COOL. MAY BE FROZEN.

TO SERVE, SPLIT SHELLS AND FILL. MAKES 40 TO 50 SHELLS

CONFUCIUS SAY: "WHO SAY I SAY ALL THOSE THINGS THEY SAY I SAY?"

INDEX
LUNCHEONS

BUFFETS

GOODIES

CAKES

APPLESAUCE SPICE CAKE—	204
BROWNIES—	205
LAZY DAISY CAKE—	207
LIGHT CHRISTMAS CAKE—	202
PRUNE CAKE—	203
SUPER CHOCOLATE CAKE	206

COOKIES

CANDIED ALMONDS—	149
CHEESE SHORTBREAD—	146
CHOCOLATE FUDGE BALLS—	150
CHOCOLATE SNOWBALLS—	148
FORGOTTEN COOKIES—	139
JEWISH SHORTBREAD—	145
MONA'S MOTHER'S MOTHER'S BEST FRIEND'S FAVORITE—	144
PECAN MACAROONS—	140
PRALINES—	143
SHORTBREAD—	145
SNOWBALLS—	148
SOFT RAISIN COOKIES—	147
SWEDISH PASTRY—	143
WHIPPED SHORTBREAD—	146

CRUSTS

CHOCOLATE WAFER CRUMB CRUST—	209
GRAHAM CRACKER CRUMB CRUST—	209
PASTRY SHELLS FOR ENTREES OR APPETIZERS—	210

DESSERTS

ANGEL FOOD FLAN—	154
ANGEL MOCHA TORTE—	152
APPLE ROLL—	156
BLUEBERRY DELIGHT—	184
BRANDIED PEACHES—	183
BRANDY SNAPS—	158
BUTTER BRICKLE DESSERT—	169
CHEESE CAKE—	151
CHERRIES JUBILEE—	168
CHOCOLATE MINT PIE—	157
CHOCOLATE MOCHA TORTE—	166
CHOCOLATE TORTE ROYALE—	180
COFFEE ICE CREAM PIE—	161
CREME DE MENTHE DESSERT—	164
FRESH STRAWBERRY PUFF PANCAKE—	172
FRUIT COCKTAIL CAKE—	160

METRIC EQUIVALENT CHART

LENGTH

1 INCH (in) = 2.5 CENTIMETERS (cm)

1 FOOT (ft.) = 30 CENTIMETERS (cm)

1 MILLIMETER (mm) = .04 INCH (in)

1 CENTIMETER (cm) = .4 INCH (in)

1 METER (m) = 3.3 FEET (ft)

MASS WEIGHT

1 OUNCE (oz.) = 28 GRAMS (g)

1 POUND (lb.) = 450 GRAMS (g)

1 GRAM (g) = .035 OUNCES (oz.)

1 KILOGRAM (kg) OR

1000 GRAMS (g) = 2.2 POUNDS (lb.)

LIQUID VOLUME

1 FLUID OUNCE (fl. oz.) = 30 MILLILITERS (ml.)

1 FLUID CUP (c.) = 240 MILLILITERS (ml.)

1 PINT (pt.) = 470 MILLILITERS (ml.)

1 QUART (qt.) = 950 MILLILITERS (ml.)

1 GALLON (gal.) = 3.8 LITERS (l.)

1 MILLILITER (ml.) = .03 FLUID OUNCES (fl. oz.)

1 LITER (l.) OR

1000 MILLILITERS = 2.1 FLUID PINTS OR

1.06 FLUID QUARTS OR

.26 GALLONS (gal.)

YOUR FAVORITES

— A GREAT GIFT IDEA! —

3029 - 3 STREET S.W.

CALGARY, ALBERTA. T2S 1V2

PLEASE SEND ME:

___ COPIES OF THE BEST OF BRIDGE AT $10.00 PER COPY.

___ COPIES OF "ENJOY!" AT $12.00 PER COPY.

PLUS $1.00 PER COPY FOR MAILING.

ENCLOSED IS $_____.

NAME_____

STREET_____

CITY_____

PROVINCE_____ POSTAL CODE_____

MAKE CHEQUE PAYABLE TO;

"THE BEST OF BRIDGE PUBLISHING LTD."

— A GREAT GIFT IDEA! —

3029 - 3 STREET S.W.

CALGARY, ALBERTA T2S 1V2

PLEASE SEND ME:

___ COPIES OF THE BEST OF BRIDGE AT $10.00 PER COPY.

___ COPIES OF "ENJOY!" AT $12.00 PER COPY.

PLUS $1.00 PER COPY FOR MAILING.

ENCLOSED IS $_____.

NAME_____

STREET_____

CITY_____

PROVINCE_____ POSTAL CODE_____

MAKE CHEQUE PAYABLE TO;

"THE BEST OF BRIDGE PUBLISHING LTD."